Invisible

to

Invincible

Invisible
to
Invincible

HOW TO CREATE A WORK CULTURE WHERE
EVERYONE FEELS LIKE A SUPERHERO

RUTH HETLAND

Soulspeak
PRESS

Published and distributed by Soul Speak Press.

Library of Congress Control Number: 2024926330
Hetland, Ruth
Invisible to Invincible: How to Create a Work Culture Where Everyone Feels Like a Superhero

ISBN 978-1-958472-17-0 (Print)
ISBN 978-1-958472-18-7 (Ebook)

To those who appreciate that true strength lies in listening, guiding, and lifting others; this book is for you. May you find encouragement in these pages and continue to uplift those around you.

Contents

Foreword   1

PROLOGUE
Invisible   3

CHAPTER 1
Origin Story: The STRONG Framework   13

CHAPTER 2
Study: Get to Know Your Team   25

CHAPTER 3
Trust: Let Your Team Know You   53

CHAPTER 4
Reinforce: Let Your Team Be Themselves   73

CHAPTER 5
Optimize: Let Your Team Shine   101

CHAPTER 6
Nurture: Be Your Team's Biggest Fan   117

CHAPTER 7
Gambol: Have Fun with Your Team   133

EPILOGUE
Invincible   153

Acknowledgments   169

Foreword

When we first met Ruth, we were immediately struck by her natural ability to inspire and lead. Over the years, we had the privilege of working closely with her and witnessing firsthand the profound impact of her leadership style. It is with great pleasure that we write this foreword for *Invisible to Invincible*.

In this book, Ruth distills the essence of what makes a truly great leader. Drawing from her experiences and understanding of human dynamics, she offers insights and practical advice that are both timeless and timely. Whether you are a seasoned executive or an aspiring leader, you will find this book to be an invaluable resource.

As Stalwart Sage, whom you'll meet later in this book, I've been inspired by Ruth's unwavering commitment to authenticity. Her leadership is a beacon of integrity, empathy, and a genuine desire to uplift others. Ruth's approach has profoundly influenced my own journey, and this book is a testament to those same values. It offers readers a heartfelt roadmap to navigate the complexities of leadership with grace and confidence, just as Ruth has shown us.

As Teamwork Titan, whom you'll also meet in these pages, it wasn't until meeting Ruth that I truly understood the transformative power of soft skills in building a great team. Though I recognized their importance, I struggled to define their value in a male-dominated industry, where these skills were sometimes seen as weaknesses. Ruth may have started as my boss, but our relationship grew into a friendship that has extended well beyond my time as her employee. It's a privilege to be part of her story and to share with you the insights that have so profoundly enriched my own journey.

It is an honor for us both to introduce you to this remarkable work and to the extraordinary leader behind it. Here's to the journey of discovery and growth this book promises.

Happy Reading!

Amanda Buth
Aka Stalwart Sage

Alycia Plattner
Aka Teamwork Titan

Invisible

The Game

"Who is ready to play *Do You Really Know Me?*" the announcer's voice echoes throughout the inside of the grain bin turned cider bar. My husband Dale and I look across the table at each other over our perfectly chilled and deliciously crisp ciders, and he says, "Should we play?" I look around the room to see what others are doing. A few people are moving toward the announcer, some clapping and whooping on their way, others dragging their feet, nudged along by their very enthusiastic partners. I don't really want to play, but the young announcer is looking right at us, pleading with his eyes for us to say yes. I shrug my shoulders. "Sure. Why not?"

We decide Dale will go first, staying at the tables grouped together for the contestants and answering questions about himself. I and the others who will try to guess our partners' answers make our way across the room and out the door, out of earshot of the announcer and his questions. As we stand outside in the brisk night air, we make light conversation and try to stay warm, some of us jumping as if an invisible rope is twirling around us. When we are finally invited back inside, we take turns guessing our partner's answers to the questions they were asked, to see if our answers match what they wrote on the small whiteboards in front of them. Many of the questions revolve around growing up, such as "Who was your favorite band growing up?" or "What was your favorite sport growing up?" Dale and I do okay; I match a few of his answers, and I miss a few. It's fun hearing everyone's answers and seeing the smiles and high fives when partners' answers match and the exaggerated frowns and playful taps when they don't.

Now it's Dale's turn to go outside and my turn to answer questions about myself. This is harder for me than answering questions about Dale because I don't like sharing things about myself, especially in a big group. When the announcer asks, "What superpower did you wish you had growing up?" my mind is suddenly blank. I quickly jot down the one thing that pops into my head: "Super Strength!" I know Dale would want to be super strong, so maybe he'll guess that about me, and besides, who wouldn't want to be super strong? We finish going through the rest of the questions, and when Dale returns, all is well until we get to the superpower question. Dale's answer shocks me. "Invisibility," he says quietly when it's his turn. He ends with a lift to his voice, as if he's asking a question, letting me know he's not very confident in his answer. I give him a curious smile, revealing my answer while simultaneously wondering why he thinks I would want to be invisible. With the game moving on, he turns to me with a whisper, as if he is Professor Charles Xavier, founder of the X-Men, and mind reading is a superpower he possesses. "I thought you would want Invisibility as your superpower because you always seem to want to stay in the background, like you don't want to be seen." I take a slow sip of my cider and ponder this as the game moves on. Yes, there were definite times growing up that I wished I was invisible, where all I wanted to do was fade into the background, like when my creepy uncle was lurking around, too close to me, or when someone dropped by unexpectedly to our almost always beyond-messy hoarder house. But what Dale said hurt me, because I knew I didn't *always* want to stay in the background, and I expected him to know that. What I wanted, always, was to be seen, truly seen, and heard and supported, which I did not feel enough of while growing up. And sometimes, I realized as I took another sip, I *really* wanted to be in the spotlight.

We finish the game and, although we are the couple who has known each other the longest, we don't win. "I guess that means we still have more to learn about each other," I smirk as we return to our seats, but I've lost interest in the rest of the evening's events. I can't stop thinking about Dale's comment. *I don't want to be invisible! How does he not know that?* I begin conjuring up a scene from the movie *Wonder Woman*, where Diana Prince, aka Wonder Woman, while standing in a foxhole amongst a group of soldiers, removes the overcoat she is wearing to reveal her armor, rope, sword, and shield. She determinedly climbs up the foxhole ladder, resisting pleas from Steve Trevor and the other men she came with, who try to convince her to stay where it is safe because she is a woman. She steps out of the foxhole and charges across no-man's-land, easily blocking fire with her bracelets and shield from the German soldiers on the other side. Steve and the other men watch in shock and awe, and only when they realize she is blocking all of the fire do they join her in her charge.

Thinking back to the game, I realize why "Super Strength!" was my gut response answer, not because I thought Dale might guess it, but because I really do want to be super strong. I've dressed up as Wonder Woman many times for Halloween, in road races, to the gym on dress-up days, and to see the *Wonder Woman* movie at the theater. I want to be like Diana. She didn't, she couldn't, stay covered, hidden, or safe. She stepped out of the background, into the light and the fire, brave and determined, driven by and leading with compassion, on a mission to protect people she had never met from the soldiers who were hurting them. She is the epitome of what it means to be super strong. And she is most definitely not afraid to be seen!

The Layoff

These days, I feel pretty strong, at least mentally. But this morning as I sit at my desk and watch the clock on my computer nearing 10:00 a.m., I feel my strength seeping out through my fingertips, evaporating across my keyboard like steam. In an attempt to lower my heart rate and calm my nerves, I take a deep breath and slowly let it out before joining the virtual meeting. I have been dreading this conversation, unsure which version of my manager will show up on the screen. I desperately hope it's the kinder one, but since I've seen less and less of him lately, I'm expecting his alter ego, the colder one. Let's call him Ironmind, the one who always gets to be right. I wonder if my team members ever feel this way before joining a meeting with me. I hope not; I try very hard to make sure they all know how much I appreciate and value them.

His face pops up in front of me on my screen before I'm ready, causing me to jump. I recognize his expression immediately, his eyes look cold and hard even through the screen, and I know it's Ironmind who is joining me. I feel myself starting to shrink into my chair. In an effort to lighten his mood, I bring up the two icebreaker topics I had thought up earlier in order to get the meeting off to a good start. He engages briefly, but I can tell he's not really interested, so I move on to the reason I scheduled this meeting. I need more information about a strategy meeting he has scheduled that will require me to travel from North Dakota to Washington, DC, in less than two weeks. He has shared next to nothing about this meeting, and I want to know what is expected of me. Before I can finish my lead-in to this topic, he interrupts me with,

"I am not prepared to have this discussion with you today, but I can't sit here and talk with you about a meeting you won't be attending." I search his emotionless face through the computer screen for more information. *Why won't I be attending the meeting?* I want to ask, but the silence is broken when he then proceeds to explain, informing me that the board has decided to stop investing in the new product we have been building, and I, along with two of my team members, will be laid off. Our last day will be next Thursday, a week from today.

Waves of dread and relief roll over me simultaneously as I absorb this news. My mind races back and forth, as if two separate voices are having an argument inside my head:

> Dread: I am losing my job!
>
> Relief: But I don't need to attend the strategy meeting I was so worried about!
>
> Dread: Two of my team members are losing their jobs!
>
> Relief: But I don't need to work for Ironmind much longer!
>
> Dread: I am losing my team!
>
> Relief: But I can stop pretending everything here is okay!

I am jolted back to the present moment when he asks me how I would like to tell my impacted team members. I shake my head in disbelief. *What? Did I hear that right? He's not actually expecting me to deliver this message to my team, is he?* I vocalize my thoughts, in a shaky voice and while I sit stiffly, waiting for his response, I become convinced that he actually does expect me to do his dirty work. "Of course not. I just want to know your thoughts on this." I agree when he suggests he schedule a meeting for the following Monday, during which he and a representative from human resources (HR) will deliver the message. He then asks me to keep this information to myself until then. *It's Thursday morning. I need to keep this to myself until Monday?* Monday feels like it might as well be next year. My head is spinning. I reluctantly agree. I know it is my only option. I have a clear moment where I think to ask if he has researched other potential roles within the organization for my two impacted team members. I don't bother to include myself in this question, already knowing his answer. He says no but agrees that's a good idea. *Why didn't that idea occur to him?* I wonder as I look for a chance to escape the rest of the conversation.

The entire meeting lasts about twenty minutes. He says he will get the Monday meeting on our calendars and thanks me for being so professional and understanding. My head feels foggy. I think I'm in shock. I don't understand so many things. I have so many questions. *Why am I being laid off but my male counterpart isn't? Why is my female team member being laid off but her male counterpart isn't? Why is my other team member, who works on multiple products, being laid off? How will this impact my other team members? Who will they report to? Who will look out for them?* I know I will not get honest answers to any of these questions, so I don't waste my energy asking them. Instead, I play the good employee and fade into the background. We both know that is what Ironmind wants. We say goodbye and I hang up, devastated for myself and every member of my team.

I immediately call Dale and blurt out the news. "I'm getting laid off!" He asks me a series of questions, which I do my best to answer in my shocked state. He's understanding, reminding me of how unappreciated I have been feeling, and reminds me that this could be a blessing in disguise, but I can tell he's also worried. We are three weeks away from buying a condo. "Will we still qualify for the short-term loan we plan to use until we can sell our house?" He assures me he will look into this as we hang up. The weight of what has just happened starts to sink in, and in the privacy of my own company I let myself finally feel it. The tears flow freely down my face as I collapse onto the floor in a heap, as if my bones are disintegrating. In a week I will be unemployed. I stare blankly at the wall.

Thankfully, I don't have any more meetings that day, and the only meetings I have the next day are optional for me; I opt not to attend. I keep my promise, except for telling Dale. It feels awful knowing about the impending doom that awaits my team, and having nowhere to take the information. As the hours and days slowly pass by, my thoughts repeat on a loop inside my weary head. *Why did he tell me? Why didn't he just ask me to postpone our meeting instead of telling me early and asking me to keep it to myself? Why hasn't he checked in on me since our meeting to see how I'm doing? Who else was involved in this decision? Who else already knows about this?*

Monday morning comes and goes, and there is no meeting request from him or from HR, even though I check for one at least fifty times. I start to wonder if the entire meeting with him was just my imagination or a terrible nightmare. I draft several messages to him but delete every one, picturing him replying with "What are you talking about?" because I imagined the whole thing. My own mind is gaslighting me. Finally, at 2:30 p.m., I can't stand it anymore and message him, "Are we having a meeting today?" I read it over at least five times before I hit send. He replies after a few agonizing moments that he's been trying to look into potential opportunities for my two team members. I sit back in disbelief. *It WAS real.* Several minutes later a meeting invite for 3:30 p.m. appears in my inbox and he messages me that he has scheduled the meeting. Immediately after, one of my team members messages me asking if I know what's up with the ominously titled meeting. I ignore him. I can't stand myself. I am such a traitor.

Just before it's time, I join the virtual meeting. I am the last person to get on the call; everyone else is ready and waiting. I peek through my webcam at my team members' nervous faces, praying they will forgive me for keeping this news from them. And then before I'm ready, Ironmind jumps right in, coldly delivering the news to my team that I have had several days to process. The message is the same. The board has decided to stop investing in the new product we have been building and we three are being laid off. Our last day will be this Thursday, three days from now. Without asking if we have questions, or taking even a moment to consider how we might be feeling, our HR representative jumps in to provide the details about our pending separation. I watch her face, cold and expressionless like Ironmind's, as she delivers the information. I study my team members' faces, watching the confusion and hurt set in as they absorb the terrible news. They sit in silence. I try to ask questions for them, knowing they are likely in shock, because I was just them a few days earlier.

Ironmind asks if we have any other questions, but starts to wrap up the meeting without giving us time to ask them. He's clearly ready to be done with us. As the meeting abruptly comes to an end, I notice one of my team members is already gone. I'm not sure at what point she dropped off. My body wants to collapse like it did a few days earlier, but I hold it together long enough to reach out to my team members. My heart aches knowing they are hurting and I am unable to heal their pain.

Weeks later while on a hike near our lake home, listening to *Dare to Lead: Brave Work. Tough Conversations. Whole Hearts.* by Brené Brown, I stop abruptly in my tracks, staring at the long winding gravel road in front of me as I absorb Brown's words:

> "Give people a 'way out with dignity'."

> "Remember the human and pay attention to feelings."

> "Keep that person who will be impacted by your decision squarely in front of you."

"Great leaders make tough 'people decisions' and are tender in implementing them. That's giving people a way out with dignity."

I rewind and listen to this section of the audiobook several times before continuing my hike, thinking back to our layoff. *Where was the dignity in that?*

The harsh reality is, we were treated as if we were already gone, even though we were expected to work through our separation date. Questions we asked about the layoff decision, our separation agreement, and our last days were answered with a clipped vagueness, devoid of any real compassion. We received no thank yous or expressions of appreciation for our contributions or tenure at the organization. We heard that our layoff had been shared with our coworkers, but we ourselves saw no evidence of this. We instead saw the opposite. In an all-company meeting the day before our separation date, the decision to stop work on the new product was announced, but nothing was said about our layoff, or us. No one from the executive leadership team or HR reached out to see how we were doing, before or after our last day.

Invisible. Invisible is how I felt from the moment the news was coldly delivered to me that Thursday morning. Invisible is how I am sure my team members felt from the moment the news was delivered just as coldly to them that Monday afternoon. Margaret Heffernan, entrepreneur, CEO, writer, and keynote speaker, wisely said, "Making those around you feel invisible is the opposite of leadership."

But invisible is *exactly* how I felt.

CHAPTER 1

Origin Story: The STRONG Framework

First Days, Part 1

I'm sitting in a room with several other new hires on our first day at a well-known and respected software company in Fargo, North Dakota. Let's call this organization Great Place Software (GPS). We were each invited to join this organization after passing a long series of intense interviews, and if the others were like me, when they received their offer, their heart leapt, a wide grin spread across their face, and they did a quick fist pump before enthusiastically saying "Yes!" As a math major who realized too late in my college career that teaching high school students was not my passion, I am so thankful to be here. I was happy to leave behind the bookkeeping role that had served me well but left me feeling uninspired at the end of each day. I am primed and ready to move into the thrilling world of software development!

The other new hires and I will be going through an intensive six-week training program together, learning the organization's software, customer service procedures, and other important topics we will need to succeed in our roles. The rest of the group will then move on to the support team, answering calls from customers about the company's software. I am different, an oddity, the first to move straight from training to a role other than support. I will move on to the development team, learning how to write and record automated tests that will verify changes developers make to the software. I am excited about this unique opportunity, but I'm also nervous, a common theme for me.

As I sit in the chair I selected, near the front, but not in the first row, I start looking through the materials placed strategically on the table in front of me. I'm going for "interested but not awkward." I'm not sure I'm executing either one very well. Tap, tap, tap, goes a finger on my shoulder. I turn around to see that a young woman with a short black bob and a wide, bright smile is the owner of the tapping finger. "Hi, I'm Diana!" My face lights up as I breathe out a sigh of relief. I easily return her smile with one of my own and introduce myself. She introduces me to another new hire, Lisa, who is sitting beside her. We talk for a few minutes and learn we have two important things in common: one, we are all newly married, and two, this is a career change for all of us. I feel my body start to relax with relief, replacing the tension it had been holding on to. I am not alone! We wrap up our brief conversation just as one of our trainers steps to the front of the room and introduces herself. As our trainers take turns sharing their stories of how they came to join and love this organization, I am filled with contentment and gratitude. *I'm going to like it here, and I already have two friends.*

Several years and many roles later, I am at a different software company. Let's call this one Not A Great Place Software (NAGPS). I am alone, sitting in a small conference room next to the huge lobby of a beautiful spacious office building, waiting anxiously for our two new hires to arrive. I came in early this morning, wanting to get settled and perhaps find a moment to calm my jittery nerves before greeting them.

It's not my first day at NAGPS, but it is my first day in my new role—I was hired as the first person in my previous role about a year ago. When we decided to expand and add more of these roles, our initial plan was to have the new hires report to the same manager I was reporting to. Then we started discussing a new leadership role, which I was offered and enthusiastically accepted. My new manager, aka Ironmind, insisted on waiting until today to communicate my promotion and make it effective, despite me requesting that at least the communication happen earlier so we could share the news with candidates. Although I was heavily involved in the hiring process, updating the job description, assembling the list of interview questions, actively participating in interviews, and providing feedback on candidates, the process was led by my previous manager, including extending offers to our two final candidates. Today, on their first day in their new roles and my first day as their manager, my initial task is to tell them they will be reporting to me, not to her, hence my jittery nerves. I really hope I don't scare them away.

I'm excited about our two new hires. One is an internal candidate with excellent product knowledge gained from roles in support and services. Let's call her Stalwart Sage. The other is an external candidate who has experience in and a passion for the Agile philosophy of project management and Scrum, the most commonly used Agile methodology. Let's call her Teamwork Titan. Together these two form the Powerhouse Pair.

As I wait for them to arrive, I reflect on how I would want news like this to be shared with me. I decided I would want my new manager to be open and honest with me, which makes my approach crystal clear. When they arrive, I greet them excitedly, then immediately share the news and watch their faces for signs of panic. Seeing none, I continue, expressing how excited I am about what each of them brings to our team and the organization. I let them absorb the news and ask questions. My goal is to make them feel welcomed and valued, and my hope is my excitement to have them here and on my team outweighs any shock or anxiety they might be feeling about having a new manager.

Work Culture

As of April 3, 2024, in Valamis's Knowledge Hub article, "Work Culture," Ivan Andreev defines work culture as "the beliefs, customs, and behavior of a group of people within a work environment; such as a team, department, or the organization as a whole. It is created through the behavior of everyone working in an organization, from the CEO to the entry-level employees." Later in the same article, Andreev defines a positive work culture as "one that prioritizes the well-being of employees, offers support at all levels within the organization, and has policies in place that encourage respect, trust, empathy, and support." Finally, he defines a toxic work culture as "one that contains dysfunctional behavior, drama, infighting, poor communication, power struggles, and low morale."

I only stayed at GPS for a year before we moved to a suburb of Saint Paul, Minnesota, for Dale's job and I had to resign. Unfortunately, remote work was not yet an option at GPS. Leaving my team was bittersweet as I looked ahead toward what other opportunities would be available to me in a bigger city. I had been working really long hours, sometimes late into the night, returning back to the office only a few hours later after taking a short nap to rejuvenate. Dale found this utterly absurd and dreadful, but I thrived on the energy of being part of a team and the commitment we all brought to a software launch. Qualities such as trust, respect, support, open and transparent communication, collaboration, teamwork, and employee recognition made the exhaustion I felt at times seem miniscule next to consistently feeling seen, heard, valued, supported, and empowered. To me, GPS was the epitome of positive work culture, and it became the standard to which I would hold every other organization.

As it turns out, I did not scare the Powerhouse Pair away from NAGPS. We ended up working closely together over the next four years, building great products and growing our team. A few months after that first day, a delightful intern temporarily joined our team. Let's call him Positivity Paladin. When we hired him full-time a few months later, the Powerhouse Pair became the Tenacious Triad. A few years later, we added another team member with mad project management skills. Let's call her Organized Oracle. With her, the Tenacious Triad morphed into the Synergy Squad. Several months later, when Stalwart Sage and Teamwork Titan left for other opportunities within a few weeks of each other, I congratulated them and wished them well, genuinely happy, knowing we had done great things together and we would maintain the strong bond we had formed for years to come. To fill their superhero shoes, we hired two new recruits: a former member of our services team who had briefly left the company and was excited to return in a new role, and an attorney who was looking to make a career transition. Let's call them Boomerang Brainiac and Counselor QuickStudy. With these two replacements, my refashioned team of four became the New Synergy Squad.

When I joined NAGPS I had high hopes that it would measure up to the standard set by GPS, and initially, it did. Unfortunately, when I came under Ironmind's direct rule, things changed significantly. I was suddenly engulfed in a negative and toxic work culture. I made it my mission to create a force field of safety around my team, prioritizing trust, respect, support, open and transparent communication, collaboration, teamwork, and employee recognition. However, outside of this protective force field, distrust, disrespect, lack of support, and poor communication loomed ominously, like nefarious elements attempting to breach Violet Parr's force fields in *The Incredibles*. Outside of my force field I frequently felt unseen, unheard, undervalued, unsupported, and powerless. I felt invisible. And then, approximately five and a half years after that first day, when I and two of my team members were so coldly laid off, it was confirmed. I had become, for all intents and purposes, invisible.

My career spans decades of work culture experience, forged by layer upon layer of professional roles spanning product management, project management, internal audit, consulting, and quality assurance, spread across several organizations in various industries. When I left GPS, I embarked on a quest, a continuous search, for a work culture that made me feel the way I had felt there. I found a few organizations that were close, and I found a few teams that were similar, but then something would happen to cause a pivotal shift, such as an acquisition, a reorganization, or both, and I no longer felt as seen, heard, valued, supported, and empowered, so I continued my quest. I even returned to GPS at one point, but not long after my return the company was acquired by a much larger organization, and a lot of things changed, including, to me most notably, the work culture. In talking with other former GPS colleagues, I know I am not alone in my quest, hearing repeatedly that once you have worked in an organization with the positive work culture GPS had, it's really hard to work someplace without it. Some found organizations that were "close enough" and settled in; some, like me, kept searching, unwilling to give up on our quest for what we once had.

I remember vividly the day I decided to write this book. I had joined the ReCLAIM Collective, a group of women led by Jessica Buchanan, *New York Times* bestselling author of *Impossible Odds: The Kidnapping of Jessica Buchanan and Her Dramatic Rescue by SEAL Team Six*. As a group, we committed to a year of concentrating on reclaiming our lives, focusing on a different area each month. I had learned some things as I did the work for January and February, but when we got to March, I couldn't wait to dig into the materials, knowing we were about to focus on reclaiming our purpose. I knew from the pull in my heart I had felt for years that I wanted more purpose in my life, but I hadn't been able to figure out yet what that looked like, and I desperately wanted to. In addition to working through the materials Jessica had provided, I ordered a journal specifically meant to help someone find work they love. The minute the package arrived on our porch, I tore it open and immediately started working through the exercises. Within the first few days of following the journal's prompts, I had come up with a short list of careers I felt drawn to: author, nonprofit executive, and life coach. I had contributed a chapter in Jessica's first anthology, *Deserts to Mountaintops: Our Collective Journey to (re)Claiming Our Voice*, so I was already a published author, and I wondered if there was more in me wanting to come out. I have served in multiple volunteer roles for various nonprofit organizations, and I was curious if a career in nonprofit was a viable option. And with my teaching degree and consulting experience, I wondered about becoming a life coach.

Included in our collective experience was a quarterly one-on-one check-in meeting with Jessica. This is when the magic happened. During our call, as I searched for the right words to explain why I was interested in these three careers, Jessica listened and asked questions, drawing out of me my unwavering interest in, and passion for, employee engagement, team building, and organizational health, which refers to the overall well-being, effectiveness, and functionality of an organization. I found myself sharing about my quest for the positive work culture I had experienced at GPS and my intentional focus on trying to recreate that culture for my team, wanting my team members to feel what I had felt: seen, heard, valued, supported, and empowered, like they could do anything. The more we talked, the more excited I became, and by the end of our meeting, I was perfectly clear on my purpose. Instead of continuing to search for the culture I had found at GPS, I would write a book about how to create more work cultures like it. I decided that if I couldn't find what I needed, I would build it, training others on how to do it, because a positive work culture shouldn't be an anomaly; it should be the standard. And that is how this book was born.

I signed on to work with Jessica as my writing coach and publisher, and as I was working on the outline for this book, I was coldly laid off by NAGPS, further confirming my purpose. Author, poet, and podcaster Bianca Sparacino insightfully said, "Sometimes, it's the people who have been hurt the most who refuse to be hardened in this world, because they would never want to make another person feel the same way they felt." This resonates with me deeply. My purpose for writing this book, my reason for sharing what I have learned working at and with a variety of organizations, is to help more people feel the way I felt at GPS: seen, heard, valued, supported, and empowered; and to never feel the way I felt at NAGPS: unseen, unheard, undervalued, unsupported, powerless, and in the end, invisible.

The Framework

We feel our most confident selves when we are able to lean into our strengths. I was many professional years into my career when I slowly came to realize and embrace the fact that my soft skills are my greatest strengths. It was as if someone inside my head was slowly turning a dimmer switch to illuminate this for me. I believe this fact is true for many people. Unfortunately, instead of leaning into these strengths, we often hide them, in an attempt to not appear weak. We have been conditioned, as a culture, to consider soft skills to be signs of weakness, when what we should be doing is embracing them for what they truly are. Active listening, appreciation, honesty, humility, respect, trust, and many other skills commonly referred to as soft skills are not soft! They are powerful skills that not everyone embodies. They are superpowers! And these superpowers are the keys to creating a positive work culture similar to GPS.

I enjoy sipping creamy, steamy coffee from a mug that bears a quote very similar to one by Cleo Wade, the legendary artist, poet, and activist: "Don't be the reason someone feels insecure. Be the reason someone feels seen, heard, and supported by the whole universe." I couldn't have designed a better mug to warm my hands and heart as I write! Shortly after purchasing this mug, I realized I have almost the same quote in my office, hanging in the center of several other framed motivational quotes. Clearly, I deeply connect with this sentiment, so it was no surprise to me when it became my inspiration for the framework I am about to share. I have organized the next six chapters around six goals that, if prioritized and supported by the essential superpowers demonstrated in each chapter, will result in creating a work culture where every single employee feels seen, heard, trusted, supported, empowered, valued, and engaged.

Below is an outline of these six goals, or what I call The STRONG Framework:

- Study: Get to Know Your Team
- Trust: Let Your Team Know You
- Reinforce: Let Your Team Be Themselves
- Optimize: Let Your Team Shine
- Nurture: Be Your Team's Biggest Fan
- Gambol: Have Fun with Your Team

I chose the six words at the beginning of each of the six goals carefully and intentionally. They each summarize the overall goal but as an added bonus, if you take the first letter of each of these words (**S**tudy, **T**rust, **R**einforce, **O**ptimize, **N**urture, **G**ambol), they form an easy to remember acronym, the word STRONG. Who doesn't feel at their best, like a superhero who can do anything, when they feel STRONG?

Below are definitions of each of these words, taken from *Dictionary.com*, to provide more context into why they were chosen for this framework:

- Study
  - "to apply oneself to acquiring a knowledge of (a subject)"
  - "to examine or investigate carefully and in detail"

- Trust
  - "to rely upon or place confidence in someone or something"
  - "to have confidence; hope"

- Reinforce
  - "to strengthen with some added piece, support, or material"

- Optimize

- "to make as effective, perfect, or useful as possible"
- "to make the best of"

- Nurture
  - "to feed and protect"
  - "to support and encourage, as during the period of training or development; foster"

- Gambol
  - "to skip about, as in dancing or playing; frolic"

In the following six chapters I provide real life examples related to each of these goals. These are my own experiences as I recall them, as an individual contributor and as a team leader, demonstrating the use (and at times the absence) of key superpowers. At the end of each chapter I include a full list of the superpowers that are key to achieving the goal, along with a few ideas on how to activate each superpower. As an added and fun bonus, each chapter concludes with a few questions for further reflection, followed by a short recap in the form of a continuing story comic strip, demonstrating the goal and relevant superpowers in use.

Lao-tzu, ancient Chinese philosopher and the traditionally accepted author of the *Tao Te Ching*, a foundational text in Taoism, observed, "Water is the softest thing, yet it can penetrate mountains and earth. This shows clearly the principle of softness overcoming hardness." I strongly believe that by leaning into our superpowers and following this framework, we can achieve these six goals and create more work cultures like GPS—positive work cultures where everyone feels like a superhero!

ORIGIN STORY

Story and illustration by Nathan Long

CHAPTER 2

Study:
Get to Know
Your Team

Study, as defined by Dictionary.com, means:

- "to apply oneself to acquiring a knowledge of (a subject)"
- "to examine or investigate carefully and in detail"

Exercises and Assessments

I remember distinctly the day I was introduced to one of my favorite leadership book authors, Patrick Lencioni, president of The Table Group and pioneer of the organizational health movement. On a bright spring morning, after dropping off our daughter at day care, I parked my car in the huge parking lot of the insurance company I had recently joined. As I made my way to the entrance, I smiled and my feet did a little jig, noticing the giant snow pile at the edge of the lot had shrunk significantly over the weekend from the warmer weather. I scanned my badge at the entrance and made my climb to the third floor, where I would weave through the maze of cubicles to my desk in the center of the audit department. As I approached my desk, I noticed something that wasn't there last night. A small, bright red book sat right in the middle of my tidy workspace: *The Five Dysfunctions of a Team: A Leadership Fable.* A yellow Post-it note with a handwritten note was perched on the cover, "Happy reading!" it said, along with a smiley face. I couldn't help but return the smile. I looked over at my teammates' desks, and noticed they had the same book with the same sticky note. I set the book aside and started unpacking my bag, meaning to ask our manager about it later, positive it was from her. A few minutes later, as my teammates were settling in, our manager popped in and confirmed my suspicions, asking with a smile that matched the sticky note if we liked our gifts. She explained that she bought the book for everyone on the team to read over the next two weeks, after which we as a team would discuss what we learned. After she left, I read the book cover again and thought, *Yikes! Are we a dysfunctional team?*

I love to read, but during my MBA program I was required to read so many leadership books that were difficult to get through I found myself reading the same paragraphs over and over trying to absorb the intended message. This experience made me averse to heavy leadership books. Not knowing if this was one of those books, I started reading it that night, unsure of how long it would take me to get through it and wanting to be sure I met our manager's goal. It didn't take me two weeks. It didn't even take me two days! I couldn't put the book down once I started reading the story of a new CEO who was taking on a team of leaders who were an absolute mess. I stayed up until the sun started to greet me, reading example after example of how the team's lack of trust and poor communication were causing impending company failure. My eyes and my brain were tired, but I couldn't stop, not until I read the last word.

Two weeks later, we gathered in the conference room for our regularly scheduled department meeting, which we all knew would be focused on the book. I couldn't wait for the meeting, having spent the last two weeks holding in my excitement after devouring the book that first night, thirsty to hear if others had the same reaction I had. I had discussed it briefly with some of my teammates, but I was looking forward to a deeper discussion with our manager and our full team. As we took our seats around the conference room table, our manager stepped up to the front of the room. She reminded us that in the book the CEO had her team attend an offsite meeting where they started off with an exercise. She then explained that we, like the CEO's team, would be answering a few personal history questions. As she handed out the sheets of paper with the questions, my heart started to race, wondering what the questions were. This was not the discussion I was expecting! I thought it would be a recap, a discussion about what we had learned, not a discussion about us. For the second time I thought, *Yikes! Are we a dysfunctional team?*

My stomach knotted up as I read through the questions on my sheet: *Number of Siblings, Hometown, Biggest Challenge Growing Up, Favorite Hobby, First Job, and Worst Job.* None of these questions were terribly threatening, but my eyes kept returning to one: Biggest Challenge Growing Up. I had huge challenges growing up. I mentally played out the scene where I shared these challenges, being very vulnerable, and I felt panic fill every part of me, from the bottom of my toes to the top of my head. Then I visualized what would happen if I shared something else, something less challenging, and I felt that panic drain away. After picturing both scenarios, I chose to play it safe and quickly jotted down answers to the questions before our time ran out. As others shared their answers, my knotted stomach began to unwind as I listened and learned more about who my teammates really were. When my turn finally came, I was relieved at how relaxed I felt as I shared that I have seven siblings, five sisters and two brothers, and my first job and worst job were the same: That time in high school where I worked at a drugstore cafe, quitting after only a few days of nearly breaking my arm from scooping rock-hard ice cream from the bottom of tubs stored in a very deep freezer.

After listening to my colleagues' heartfelt answers, I briefly considered reversing my decision to play it safe and to be very vulnerable with Biggest Challenge Growing Up, but I instantly felt that panic start to return, so I played it safe. I stuck with my written answer, in the same theme of Worst Job, sharing how hard it was to be vertically challenged. This wasn't really the truth, but I just couldn't bring myself to share my actual biggest challenges growing up. I wasn't ready. I held onto both of those for many more years, finally sharing in *Deserts to Mountaintops: Our Collective Journey to (re)Claiming Our Voice*.

After everyone had taken a turn sharing their answers, our manager thanked us for reading the book, sharing a bit about our personal histories, and helping her learn more about us. She then ended the meeting. As we got up to leave the conference room, instead of rushing back to our desks like we normally did, we walked slowly, talking and asking each other more questions as we wove our way back through the maze of cubicles to our desks. The exercise had successfully whetted our appetite for more information about each other. Our manager had leaned into her ***desire to learn*** and ***friendliness*** superpowers, getting to know us better and helping us get to know each other better, not only during the exercise but after it ended.

A few weeks after this exercise, our manager arranged for us to take the Myers-Briggs Type Indicator (MBTI) assessment, a personality assessment that groups people into one of sixteen categories. We again gathered as a team in the conference room, but this time instead of sharing stories with each other, we sat quietly, completing the assessment, answering questions based on four categories of preferences: extroverted versus introverted, sensing versus intuiting, thinking versus feeling, and judging versus perceiving.

When our assessment results came back, we returned to the conference room once again to review them as a team. Our manager had brought in a consultant for this step, who was walking around the big conference room table handing out our individual reports. When she got to me, I was so excited to see what my report said, I almost gave her a paper cut because I grabbed it so quickly from her. I gave her a timid smile and apologized, then scanned through the pages. The report said my preference is ISFJ (introverted, sensing, feeling, judging), described as the practical helper. People with ISFJ preferences have a natural drive to understand the needs of others and use this understanding to figure out exactly how to care for the people around them. ISFJs tend to be responsible and practical; they often value common sense. They enjoy helping others and leaving things better than how they found them. I looked up from my report, unable to contain the smile spreading across my face. That was me to a T! I felt so seen!

We spent the rest of our meeting time reviewing our reports together, with the consultant leading our discussion. I sat entranced as she shared examples of how, by understanding our different preferences, we could work better together as a team. At the end of the meeting, as we got up to leave the conference room, it was as if we had stepped back in time to after we shared our personal histories a few weeks earlier. We continued talking, wanting to learn even more about each other and our different preferences as we followed the maze back to our desks. Our manager had again leaned into her ***desire to learn*** superpower, to get to know us even better and in a different way, while helping us all do the same.

———————————

A few years later, a hiring manager asked me during an interview to tell him about my strengths and weaknesses. After I finished answering, he pulled the book, *StrengthsFinder 2.0: Discover Your CliftonStrengths* by Tom Rath, from the bookshelf behind him. He said he and his team were reading it and taking the included assessment, CliftonStrengths, which reveals an individual's top five of thirty-four strength areas. After the interview, excited to learn more, I drove straight to our local Barnes & Noble bookstore to search the shelves for the book. When I found it I skimmed through the pages covering the thirty-four strength areas. I wanted to hug the author, falling in love with the idea behind the book, that individuals should focus on their strengths rather than their weaknesses to achieve personal and professional success. I quickly made my way to the counter to purchase it, carefully meandering through the other customers scanning books between the towering bookshelves. Several days later I received a call from the hiring manager, and he offered me the job. Joy bubbled up from inside me and burst out as I accepted. I couldn't wait to work for someone who had given me such a gift, the introduction to a book that spoke so clearly to me.

A few weeks later, before our first one-on-one meeting, I grabbed my book from my backpack and walked to his office, excited to show him I was a team player. I did not receive the reaction I was expecting. When I showed him the book it was as if I had been transported to a different, darker universe. He seemed to change right before my eyes. This was my first glimpse of this version of him, where his smile disappeared and his face took on a harsh, disapproving scowl. Annunciating precisely and with finality, he said, "We are finished with that exercise." I didn't know how to respond. I somehow got through the rest of the meeting and when it was over, I slunk back to my cubicle, with my shoulders hunched forward, confused and disheartened. I thought he had brought up the book in the interview because he wanted to learn more about me and my strengths! I slumped into the chair back at my desk and wondered, *Should I not have bought the book?* Followed by, *Should I not have accepted his offer?*

After some reflection back at my desk, I convinced myself that he was probably just having a bad day. I hadn't taken the assessment yet so I decided to proceed and share my results with him in our next one-on-one meeting. As I worked through the assessment that evening however, I kept seeing his face and I questioned every response, wondering if he would expect me to answer it differently. I bit my lower lip, worrying, *What if my results don't show strengths he respects?* I started to doubt my plan to share my results with him. When I finally finished the assessment I felt better, at first. My report outlined the five strength areas I scored highest in: Input, Individualization, Learner, Achiever, and Empathy, along with information on how to leverage these five strengths. I didn't disagree with the results, but deep down I wondered, *Are these really my top five strengths, or were the results tainted by me letting him get inside my head?*

I brought my report with me to our next one-on-one meeting, but when I mentioned taking the assessment to my manager, I was once again transported to that different, darker universe. He curtly reminded me that he was finished with that exercise. Feeling hurt and deceived, I carefully tucked my report back inside my notebook, hoping he hadn't noticed I had brought it. Like before, I somehow got through the rest of that meeting, and when it was over, I skulked back to my desk and hid my report, realizing he wasn't having a bad day before. This was him, and I had met someone else during the interview. I understood. The book was bait, something to lure me in, and I had swallowed it whole. He wasn't interested in my strengths, and he wasn't interested in getting to know me. I sat at my desk feeling unseen, unheard, and unsafe. Let's call him Frostgrip, the one with the icy touch. You will see him again.

Several years later I decided to retake the CliftonStrengths assessment, curious to see if my results would differ from the assessment I took in those early days under Frostgrip's rule. This time as I took the assessment I didn't question my responses. This report showed all thirty-four CliftonStrengths, in rank order. Input had moved down in the list, to eight, and Achiever had moved even further down, to twenty-two. Moving up to replace them in the top five were Developer and Relator, making my top five strengths Individualization, Empathy, Developer, Learner, and Relator. This top five felt more like me, a clear representation of my superpowers.

———————————

One of the tools Jessica recommended to our collective during the month I reclaimed my purpose was the Enneagram, which is a philosophy that centers around nine temperament types. She encouraged each of us to take a free assessment to determine our temperament type using a link she provided. I took the assessment, and I tested out as a type nine, The Peacemaker. Nines are honest and peaceful people who want to live free in a harmonious environment. Bringing people together and sharing experiences is something Nines are good at. At first I wasn't excited about this result, as Nines tend to avoid conflict, but I had to agree; it sounds just like me!

After taking the Enneagram assessment, I decided to lean into my own *desire to learn* and *friendliness* superpowers and I shared the link, along with my result, with my team members. I waited in anticipation for my team members to share their own results, excited to learn more about them. Almost everyone joined in and shared their result. Jessica had not only provided a way for our collective to learn more about ourselves and each other; she had also provided a fun way for me to learn more about my team!

Moves

Through several years of circling the city of Saint Paul as nomads, moving from suburb to suburb, apartment to apartment, Dale and I developed a love for the city and knew this was where we wanted to buy our first home. Before we could though, we needed to save up money for a down payment, so we downsized, renting a small apartment in a big old house in a cool old neighborhood of Saint Paul, two blocks from historic Summit Avenue and within walking distance of some of our favorite restaurants and the homemade ice cream shop where we became known as regulars. We were both pursuing our MBAs, in a bit of a race to see who would finish first. I had started my program two years before Dale, but because my undergrad was in mathematics and his was in business, I had a longer track to complete my MBA than he did. I had been keeping a slow, steady pace balancing one class a week with the consulting job I had landed almost immediately after we moved to the area, which required some out-of-town travel. When I realized Dale would finish way before me if I stuck to my current pace, I panicked, not wanting to fall behind, and quickened my pace to match his, taking two classes per semester, which would allow us to get to the finish line at the same time. This unfortunately meant I would need to look for a different role, one that didn't require travel and would allow me to consistently attend classes two nights a week.

I found a new role in the Information Technology (IT) department of a huge hospital system, and once we had saved enough money, we purchased a cute little bungalow in a quiet neighborhood several blocks from the big, old house we had been renting, within walking distance of some of our other favorite restaurants. Shortly after purchasing this new-to-us old home, I learned that GPS had opened an office in a suburb of Saint Paul. A plan began brewing, a way for us to move back to Fargo after we graduated with our MBAs. We had also recently learned that my oldest brother, who lived just west of Fargo, had been diagnosed with amyotrophic lateral sclerosis (ALS), commonly known as Lou Gehrig's disease. A transfer within GPS back to Fargo would allow us the opportunity to be closer to him and his family, to help them as his muscles lost their ability to understand his nerves signaling when to move.

I did rejoin GPS, and about two years later, on a bitterly cold December afternoon, everyone in our office squeezed into the conference room to connect with the Fargo team for a big company announcement. As I heard the news that GPS would soon be acquired by a much larger software company, my heart raced in both excitement and worry, concerned about the impact this might have on the company's positive work culture. A few weeks later, Dale and I had completed our MBA race and, in the middle of a blizzard that can only be experienced in places like Minnesota and North Dakota, we packed up our belongings and said goodbye to the cute little bungalow in Saint Paul, carefully making our way back to Fargo to another old house.

I didn't notice many changes at first, but as the acquisition progressed, I noticed movement, a lot of movement, of me. About a year after we moved back to Fargo, I started in a new role just before having our daughter. When I returned from maternity leave several weeks later, I had the same manager as I had before I left. Then the movement started. I was moved to a different manager every few months as the company tried on reorganization after reorganization. I felt like a murder suspect in the game Clue, a game piece that people kept picking up and moving to a different room. One afternoon I was sitting at my desk when I received yet another summons to a conference room with very little notice. I was pretty sure I knew what was coming as I walked to the conference room, resigned to hearing news of yet another reorganization. But this time was different. This time when I heard the news it felt like I had been kicked in my stomach. I tried to listen as our leadership team explained the new organizational chart, but all I could focus on was that I was not only moving away from my current manager, who made me feel safe and supported, but I would be moving to someone who made me feel the exact opposite: unsafe and insecure. My to-be manager was someone I actively avoided as much as possible, having seen her treat several people in meetings like they were below her and unworthy of her time when they disagreed with her or offered suggestions. Let's call her Stoneheart, the one with no empathy.

I had to have heard that wrong! It made no sense! She had no experience in our area! How was she going to support me? But I knew deep down I had heard it exactly right. The weight of this awful news on top of what I was already carrying as a relatively new mom whose brother was slowly dying was too much. I had to get out of that room! I pushed back my chair and mumbled what I knew wasn't an adequate apology but was all I could manage in my rush to get out the door and to the nearest bathroom before bursting into tears. I barely made it. A few minutes later my manager found me in a crumpled mess against one of the bathroom walls, trying desperately to get control of my emotions but failing miserably. She came over and sat on the floor beside me, close but not too close, and listened as I sobbed out everything I was feeling. She knew I was a new mom, as she was, and she knew about my brother's disease and prognosis. She had learned these things through one-on-one conversations, using her ***active listening***, ***asking questions***, and ***desire to learn*** superpowers to get to know me. As I sobbed, she listened and responded in quiet, soothing tones. She told me that she understood, and she assured me that she would still be there for me as much as I needed her. She leaned into her superpowers of **compassion**, **empathy**, and **respect**, making me feel seen and heard, not embarrassed, or judged. I took a deep breath, wiped my tears, and thanked her. Then we walked back to the conference room together.

Several weeks later, in a one-on-one meeting with Stoneheart, I was trying to explain an issue I was having with one of my projects. I was struggling, because instead of listening, she kept interrupting me, trying to give me advice without fully understanding the issue. She was, before my eyes, confirming and recreating the fear that had caused my meltdown weeks earlier. After being rudely interrupted for the twentieth time, I became so frustrated and flustered I blurted out the first thing that came to mind, something that was lurking but wasn't meant to escape: "Maybe this isn't the right role for me!" She looked at me with a cold, intent stare and said, "Maybe you're right." I left her office a few minutes later, feeling distraught, dismissed, and alone.

Thankfully, not long after this one-on-one meeting I received another conference room summons, announcing yet another reorganization. As I walked to the conference room this time, I silently prayed to be moved to a different manager. My prayer was answered a few minutes later when I learned I was moving to someone who did have experience in our area. I couldn't stop the grin spreading across my face, then quickly glanced at Stoneheart, concerned she had seen me. Thankfully, her attention was fully on the speaker in front of us. A warm wave of relief washed over me. I was safe.

Even though my impression of him had always been positive, as I walked to my first one-on-one meeting with my new manager, my heart was racing. I kept flashing back to my last one-on-one meeting with Stoneheart, thinking, *What if this one ends the same way?* When I sat down across from him, he asked me how things were going, and I could see from his expression and hear in his voice that he wasn't just asking; he really wanted to know. This small gesture of empathy released a floodgate of emotions I had been holding back, and tears started streaming from my eyes. I was mortified and quickly apologized, expecting him to freak out, but he didn't. He sat quietly until he could tell I was ready to speak, then he asked me questions to understand the issue I was having with my project. After several minutes of us talking through my situation, including me hesitantly sharing about my previous one-on-one and how I worried this wasn't the right role for me, he acknowledged that I was working with a project team and on a project that would be challenging for someone with years of experience. He told me he wanted to see me be successful in my role. He didn't judge me. He didn't dismiss me. He saw me, and he heard me. Within two weeks that project was reassigned, and I was able to focus on my other projects, which were much more aligned with my background and skills. He had leaned into his superpowers of ***active listening***, ***asking questions***, ***compassion***, and ***empathy*** to get to know me and to help me be successful.

One-on-One Time

When I took on my leadership role at NAGPS, having experienced one-on-one time with managers who wanted to get to know me, I knew I wanted this for my team members. One way I knew to do this was through a regularly scheduled one-on-one meeting. Before scheduling one-on-one meetings with Stalwart Sage and Teamwork Titan, I sought feedback from them on how often they wanted to meet. Knowing our roles involved a lot of meetings already, I didn't want to overload their schedules. We discussed this together and decided to have one-on-one meetings every other week. On the opposite weeks, we would meet as a team.

I wanted these meetings to be about them, to talk about whatever they needed to talk about. We had no set agenda, but after seeing a LinkedIn post from Claire Lew, CEO of Canopy, sharing a list of questions to ask during a one-on-one meeting, I added several of them to our meeting invite, in case we needed a prompt:

1. How's life?
2. What are you worried about right now?
3. What rumors are you hearing that you think I should know about?
4. What are your biggest time wasters?
5. Would you like more or less direction from me?
6. Are there any decisions you're hung up on?

Sometimes I would have my own topics to discuss, but I waited to bring these up until after my team members had gone through their topics. As we expanded our team, I carried this same cadence and structure forward to one-on-one meetings with my new team members.

In the beginning when one of my team members would raise a concern or an issue, I would immediately try to help them solve it, thinking that as their manager I had to have all the answers. I quickly learned this wasn't the right approach, for me or for them. I needed to listen more than I spoke, leaning into my *active listening* and *asking questions* superpowers. By listening attentively and asking follow-up questions instead of offering suggestions, I would usually find that when they raised a concern or an issue, they already had a plan, or at least an idea, about what to do. What they were looking for was confirmation and support. If they didn't already have a plan or an idea in mind, asking them questions and brainstorming solutions with them almost always led to them coming up with their own solution. This felt better to me than offering them a solution, knowing they had a part in defining it.

I enjoyed using this time with my team members to learn more about them, both professionally and personally. Our meetings weren't always focused on work, which I appreciated and encouraged. They often included catching up about fun events they had attended, exercise plans or injuries, and news about their kids, families, weekends, and vacations. I wanted my team members to know I cared about more than their work. I cared about them, and I enjoyed learning about their lives.

On the topic of learning about their lives, I will never forget how I messed up terribly with one of my team members in this area. At a work gathering after having one-on-one meetings with my team earlier that week, I shared news with someone that a team member had shared with me. Although the news was something she would eventually have shared, it was not *my* news to share. Then I shared the news *again*, also sharing a judgmental comment that someone made at the work gathering. This got back to my team member, who asked to meet with me. When we met, and she shared with me that she had heard I had shared her news not just once, but twice, and made a judgmental comment, my first reaction was to clarify. I attempted to explain that it wasn't me who had made the judgmental comment, and that I had shared the news because I was excited for her, but as I said it and watched her eyes fill with disappointment, I realized I had completely missed her point. I wished I was Doctor Strange and could use the Time Stone to rewind time to before I had shared her news, or at least to the beginning of this conversation. Instead, I did what I could do. I acknowledged that I had made a terrible mistake by sharing news that wasn't mine to share, and I apologized. Although she thanked me for owning my mistake and assured me that we were okay, I knew it would take time to repair our relationship after my breach of confidence.

Several months after this, a few weeks after my first hiking epiphany, I was on another hike, again listening to *Dare to Lead*. In this chapter, Brown shared about the BRAVING Inventory elements, seven behaviors that define trust: Boundaries, Reliability, Accountability, Vault, Integrity, Nonjudgement, and Generosity. This is a tool she uses with her team, having each person fill out a BRAVING Inventory, then meeting one-on-one to discuss where individual experiences align and where they differ. Hearing her description of Vault hit me like a ton of bricks: "You don't share information or experiences that are not yours to share."

I told my team members frequently that if they needed something from me in between our one-on-one meetings that I was available for them, whenever they needed me. I knew it was important for me to be there for them. I wanted them to feel seen and heard.

One afternoon as I was quietly working at my desk, one of my team members asked me if we could talk. When we met a few minutes later, she looked nervous, looking down instead of at me and not smiling as she usually did, so I knew she was dealing with something important. I listened carefully as she shared that she had been talking with another company and was debating taking a role with them. As I listened, I could feel myself starting to panic. I tried to silence the voice in my head screaming, "No! You can't let her go!" I took deep breaths, inhaling and exhaling slowly, trying to appear calm. I asked her a few questions about the role and the organization, trying to understand what she was thinking and feeling, because she hadn't told me she was leaving, and her face didn't look like someone excited about taking on a new role.

She, of course, may have been masking her excitement to protect my feelings. I asked her what was drawing her to this other company and role. She didn't mention salary, which surprised me. Instead, she said she didn't really want to leave, but they were offering her more time off. I knew her personal time was very important to her, so I ignored the negative voice in my head telling me she won't stay anyway, thanked her for coming to me, and asked her if she could give me some time to investigate getting her an extra week off. She said okay, but her clenched hands and shaky voice told me she was worried this wouldn't turn out well for her. I was worried, too, about how Ironmind would react. But I had to try. She needed to know I had her back.

I set up a meeting with Ironmind because I needed his permission to offer her another week. As I started to update him on our discussion, he interrupted me, assuming she was trying to use this other opportunity to get a raise, which he firmly stated we would not give her. I clarified that we had only discussed time off, not salary. He was convinced offering her another week of time off wouldn't satisfy her, but he challenged me to try. I went back to her and offered her the additional week, which she happily accepted. She thanked me for listening to her, caring about her needs, and pushing to get her the extra week. Leaning into my superpowers of **active listening**, **asking questions**, **compassion**, **empathy**, and **reading body language** had allowed me to leverage what I already knew about her as well as learn what she really needed from me. And she stayed, proving both the negative voice in my head and Ironmind wrong.

My one-on-one meetings with Ironmind were not something I looked forward to. I dreaded them, knowing I would leave feeling the exact opposite of how I wanted my team members to feel after our one-on-one meetings. These meetings were not about me; they were about Ironmind, to talk about whatever was on *his* mind. He spoke way more than he listened, and he rarely made eye contact, constantly looking away, at his other screen or down, I assume at his phone. When I did try to talk, I felt dismissed as he interrupted, corrected, and sometimes belittled me. I learned to be very careful, only saying what I thought he wanted to hear, after experiencing too many times to count his criticism of me, my current and previous team members, and others during these meetings. To this day, I wonder what he said about me to others.

Every few months our one-on-one meetings would fall off my calendar, and I would do a little dance. Then reality would hit me and I would realize if I didn't reach out to Ironmind to get them reestablished, somehow this would be seen as my fault. I never understood why he didn't set up the recurring meeting with no expiration date. He might not have known how, but I knew better than to offer to show him; he did not welcome suggestions.

Team Time

One of the things I appreciated most about working at a corporation that owned several operating companies was the time we spent together as a team when traveling. Our audit team traveled several times a year to conduct audits at these operating companies, and we also traveled a few times to attend conferences. During these trips we worked (or learned) hard during the day, but our manager made sure we always went out for dinner together in the evening. I remember one particularly hard day at one of our operating companies in Prince Edward Island, Canada. We were planning to go out with a group of operating company leaders for a fresh lobster dinner, a unique opportunity we didn't have living in Fargo, but I was behind on my audit, so I had asked to stay behind at the hotel to work. Our manager didn't want me to miss out, insisting I go. She knew I was worried about finishing my audit, having skipped the lobster boat excursion the rest of the audit team had experienced earlier. She assured me that I would have time to finish the audit the next day, and after a few more attempts to change her mind, I reluctantly gave in.

Later that night I enjoyed freshly caught mussels and lobster, creamy potatoes, and crisp vegetables, all oozing with hot melted butter, but what I enjoyed most was the fun conversation I had with my teammates and the operating company leaders. Across the table from me, as our manager smiled with her eyes and chuckled boisterously, it was easy to see she enjoyed having this time with her team, and I couldn't help but smile as the warmth of feeling seen and heard engulfed me. She had understood that I needed this when I myself hadn't understood what I needed. I was relatively new to auditing, and without this outing I would have spent the entire evening in my hotel room alone, worrying about the next day, reviewing and unnecessarily tweaking my audit plan, and getting very little sleep. Dinner out got my mind off work for a while and helped me relax, leading to better sleep that night and a fresh focus the next day to finish my audit. I appreciated our manager leaning into her *compassion*, *desire to learn*, and *friendliness* superpowers to encourage me to join our audit team that evening. These team outings helped us relax and have fun together after a long and sometimes hard day. Although I didn't catch on immediately, they became something I looked forward to, especially knowing our manager enjoyed spending this extra time with us, getting to know each of us better.

A few months after our first day together as a team at NAGPS, the Powerhouse Pair and I attended an out of town conference together. I wanted my team members to experience what I had felt traveling with my audit team, spending time together getting to know each other outside of the office. We attended separate breakout sessions, but we made sure to sit together at mainstage sessions and at lunch. We also participated in evening activities together, including one night that we dressed up as lumberjacks in red plaid shirts and posed outside in the snow and behind an ice sculpture, laughing later when we realized in every photo taken throughout the entire conference we were, without realizing it, standing in the exact same order. This extended time together let us relax and have fun, bonding as a team. It gave my two new team members time to be themselves, away from work, and I learned a lot about them during this trip that I might not have learned (or learned as quickly) without spending that time together. I really enjoyed attending this conference and others with my team members and leaning into my *desire to learn* and *friendliness* superpowers during our free time to get to know them better.

As I mentioned earlier, I held regular team meetings with my team every other week, on the opposite weeks of our one-on-one meetings. When I created my first team meeting agenda, I knew I wanted to carry forward a tool I had used in previous roles, a gem I had pocketed several years earlier while attending the Dale Carnegie Course. Over the span of several weeks my coursemates and I were immersed in learning the principles covered in Dale Carnegie's books *How to Win Friends and Influence People* and *How to Stop Worrying and Start Living*, summarized in our workbooks and the tiny copies of *Dale Carnegie's Golden Book* we each received our first day. Each week we took turns standing in front of our coursemates, sharing challenges we were facing in our professional and personal lives and how we were applying what we were learning in the course to those challenges. We were encouraged to be vulnerable, knowing we would not be judged, but met instead with encouragement, support, and respect. A vivid memory for me was one coursemate who started his speech with, "I love my wife," his voice breaking as he said it. My heart ached and my eyes filled with tears as he swallowed, took a deep breath, and continued, sharing his very personal story of an illness his wife was battling. The bonds we formed as we were vulnerable and raw in front of each other were a surprising benefit of taking the course. When we left our last session, I felt grief, like I was leaving my closest friends, something I had not expected when I signed up for the course.

One of the tools I took from the course, the gem I mentioned above, was how we started each session. Before we dove into our coursework, we gave everyone an opportunity to share good news. It was optional, and it didn't take much time, but it relaxed everyone and allowed those who wanted to share an experience the opportunity to do so. It didn't need to be course related; it just needed to be good news. I enjoyed hearing the good news and congratulating the person sharing it and seeing others do the same.

While attending the Dale Carnegie Course I was working at a hospitality company, and I was excited to apply this tool to our project meetings. Before I implemented it, I wanted to be sure our project sponsor was in agreement. I was pretty sure he would be, as he was all about team building. As I described the idea to him, explaining how we were using it in the Dale Carnegie Course, his eyes lit up and he excitedly agreed, "Let's do it!"

Good News became our first agenda item for every project team meeting. When we introduced it to the project team, we reinforced that it was optional and it did not need to be work related. We kicked things off by sharing our own good news. I shared about completing a long run for an upcoming relay race I was training for, a simple personal example to help others feel comfortable sharing and so they knew it didn't need to be work related. The team quickly embraced this tool, never having a shortage of good news to share. This quick agenda item allowed me to get to know my project team members better and started our meetings off on a happy, friendly note, making them much more fun and interactive. Seeing its success with this project team, I carried it forward, adding it to the agenda for other project team meetings I led.

I added Good News to the top of the agenda for our first team meeting at NAGPS, and when we met, Stalwart Sage suggested we include Best Professional/Best Personal, a similar concept she had seen used in other team meetings. I had seen this used too, but it had been required, and I wanted ours to be optional. With this compromise we added it, forming Good News/Best Professional/Best Personal. This became one of my favorite parts of our team meetings. I loved learning more about my team members by celebrating their good news and achievements. It also gave me an opportunity to bring up and celebrate professional accomplishments they may have forgotten to mention. When introducing the agenda item, I would lean into my ***desire to learn*** and ***friendliness*** superpowers, smiling and asking with genuine enthusiasm, "Who has some good news or best professional or best personal items to share?" Most of the time at least one person had a story they wanted to share with the team. I reinforced that this was optional, respecting that not everyone is as comfortable sharing as others, by not calling on anyone directly. If there wasn't anything to share, I would continue, but often as we moved through the rest of the agenda, someone would think of something they had forgotten to mention. I kept notes of these items and would go back up to add it. These notes became a great tool for me to look back on during performance reviews, a record of my team members' accomplishments in their own words. As I had hoped, this tool started our meetings on a friendly, positive note and helped us get to know each other better, becoming a standing agenda item throughout my tenure.

Another standing agenda item in our team meetings was Status Updates. This was a suggestion from Teamwork Titan, which I happily adopted. Each team member would provide an update on what we had been working on, what work we had coming up, and any challenges we were facing. I provided my own update, but mostly I listened and asked questions. I took notes as team members provided their updates, so this also became a great tool for me to look back on during performance reviews. What I loved to see happen during these meetings was a team member bringing up a challenge they were facing, followed by the team asking questions to try to better understand and work through the challenge together. Sometimes these were easy things like how to do something in Excel or another tool we used. Sometimes they were more complex and required more discussion or another meeting to dive in deeper. What I saw was that no one was alone; we were there to help each other, wanting everyone to be our best selves, to feel seen and heard. This was a direct benefit of getting to know my team and helping them get to know each other, and this is why I call them the Synergy Squad and the New Synergy Squad.

Led by Ironmind, our leadership team meetings, like my one-on-one meetings with Ironmind, were not something I looked forward to. These meetings did not have an agenda, or a set cadence. We sometimes attempted small talk at the beginning of the meeting, but any attempts from Ironmind to get to know us better were surface level at best and quickly shifted back to him. I always sat teetering on the edge of my chair, on edge myself, never knowing if I would be called on to provide an update. Thankfully, I was always prepared, having my team meeting notes to reference, but I was always waiting for the interruption, eye roll, or criticism that I experienced on a regular basis. Most of the time, to my relief, we just listened to him provide updates. He didn't want discussion. He only wanted agreement. This was evident in how he brought up a topic as if he wanted to get our opinions, but then it would come, the inevitable "Right?" or "Don't you agree?" immediately slamming the discussion door.

STUDY SUPERPOWERS

Superpower	Activation
Active Listening	To lean into my ***active listening*** superpower, I try to eliminate distractions around me, giving my full attention to the person speaking. This helps me focus on them and their words. I show them that I am engaged and interested by using nonverbal cues; for example, maintaining eye contact, nodding, and changing my facial expressions. To make sure I fully understand the message, I paraphrase what the person is saying and encourage them to elaborate to gain further understanding.
Asking Questions	I lean into my ***asking questions*** superpower by being curious and genuinely interested in what the other person is saying. By asking open-ended and follow-up questions, I encourage a deeper level discussion. While actively listening to the person speaking, I wait for natural pauses to ask questions that will deepen the conversation.
Compassion	By leaning into my ***compassion*** superpower, I foster an environment where people feel safe expressing themselves by actively listening to their concerns, acknowledging their feelings, and offering my support. I show genuine interest in getting to know people beyond their roles. I also acknowledge and celebrate their strengths and achievements.

Superpower	Activation
Desire to Learn	I lean into my ***desire to learn*** superpower by showing genuine curiosity about people, both in their professional and personal lives. I ask questions about their interests and goals and encourage them to share their insights and perspectives. I pay attention to details shared during conversations and follow up on previous discussions.
Empathy	To lean into my ***empathy*** superpower, I create a supportive environment where people feel understood and valued by sensing and validating their emotions. I actively listen without interrupting and focus on being fully engaged in the conversation. I find that withholding judgment and providing emotional support instead of immediately suggesting solutions fosters deeper connections and trust.
Friendliness	Greeting others with a warm smile and maintaining positive eye contact helps me embody my ***friendliness*** superpower. I like to address people by their names and actively seek personal connections. In addition, expressing enthusiasm, maintaining an approachable demeanor, and engaging in active listening help me demonstrate genuine friendliness and encourage positive interactions.
Reading Body Language	To lean into my ***reading body language*** superpower, I pay close attention to changes in facial expressions to help me accurately interpret emotional cues. I observe body posture and gestures to gain insight into underlying feelings and reactions. In addition, I monitor eye contact and personal space to gauge how comfortable and engaged a person is.

Superpower	Activation
Respect	I lean into my *respect* superpower by focusing on being polite and courteous in my interactions. I allow people to express themselves without interrupting them, to let them know that I value their thoughts and opinions. Most importantly, I avoid criticizing, judging, shaming, and humiliating anyone.

STUDY WRAP-UP

Jack Welch, the legendary writer, speaker, and former chairman and CEO of General Electric (GE), is known for this sage advice: "Take time to get to know people. Understand where they are coming from, what is important to them. Make sure they are with you." This quote embodies the spirit of this chapter. By leaning into your superpowers of *active listening*, *asking questions*, *compassion*, *desire to learn*, *empathy*, *friendliness*, *reading body language*, and *respect* to get to know your team, you will create an environment where everyone feels seen and heard.

STUDY REFLECTION

1. Which superpowers really stood out to you in this chapter?
2. Which of these superpowers are most natural for you?
3. Which of these superpowers are most challenging for you?
4. Which story or stories in this chapter did you most relate to?
5. Which story or stories did you least relate to?
6. Which superpowers were missing in the interactions with Frostgrip, Ironmind, and Stoneheart?

7. Has a team member ever shared something personal with you? How did you respond?

8. What are some ways you can Study: Get to Know Your Team?

CHAPTER 3

Trust:
Let Your Team
Know You

Trust, as defined by Dictionary.com, means:

- "to rely upon or place confidence in someone or something"
- "to have confidence; hope"

First Days, Part 2

As I sit in the small conference room next to the huge lobby of the beautiful spacious office building and wait for the Powerhouse Pair to arrive, I shift in my seat, crossing, then uncrossing my legs in an attempt to stop my heels from bouncing up and down. Shifting works temporarily, until it doesn't, and the movement returns all on its own, like an unwelcome guest that keeps appearing unexpectedly at my front door after I ask them repeatedly to leave. I am not sure how much I should share with my new team members. *Should I tell them this is my first leadership role, and that they will be my first direct reports? Will this scare them? Will they respect me if I am open and honest with them?* As I continue to shift in my chair, I think back to one of my first days at the hospitality company and realize I might have my answer.

Our project management department was brand new, and we were its inaugural team members. Our manager had gathered us together and openly admitted that although she had served in several project manager-type roles and managed many, many projects, she had never established a project management function. Then she asked for our help. She told us in addition to serving as project managers, she would appreciate having our help in establishing the project management function by helping define our processes and procedures. If she was nervous about delivering this message, I saw no signs of it, but she had absolutely no reason to be nervous. I saw this as an opportunity! I could dig deep into my project management experience and training and leave my mark here with clearly defined processes and procedures! I loved that she was so transparent in sharing this with us, and that she so openly asked for our help. I told her I was thrilled to be part of building this with her, and my teammates responded with similar enthusiasm. Our manager had leaned into her **honesty**, **openness**, and **transparency** superpowers and trusted us with something she could have kept to herself and probably done by herself. Instead she invited us to help her, and we excitedly accepted.

My heel bouncing and seat shifting has slowed down, and I reflect back to other managers to whom I have reported, some good, and some bad.

The good managers, the ones I have felt most connected to, including the one at the hospitality company, let me see them as more than my manager, by openly sharing stories about their personal lives, families, and interests outside of work. They let me into their humanity. The good managers leaned into their *vulnerability* superpower, sharing challenges they had faced or were facing, enabling me to trust them and to feel safe sharing my own challenges with them. The managers I have felt least connected to always seemed to be guarded, sharing few details about their personal lives, and never opening up about their challenges. If there was any sort of exchange with these managers related to their personal lives or a challenge, it came across as a brag, not as a way to connect and build trust.

My heel bouncing and seat shifting has stopped. I have my answer: I want to be one of the good managers. I visualize myself excitedly sharing personal and professional updates with Stalwart Sage and Teamwork Titan, responding to their questions with transparency, admitting to them when I don't know something, and sharing not only my successes but also my failures, hoping they will learn from my mistakes. I want my team members to know me, trust me, and feel safe with me, because I know how good this feels, and I know how bad it feels when that is missing.

I sit back in my chair and smile, knowing I have come to the right decision: I will be transparent with Stalwart Sage and Teamwork Titan and let them know this is my first leadership role and they will be my first direct reports. I will also ask for their help in establishing the product management function. For a moment my heel bouncing returns as I consider what it might look like if they react differently than our project management team did, picturing them looking back at me in confusion, frustration, and anger, but after a few deep breaths I decide it's worth the risk. I will start things off right, by being open and honest with them, not hiding the truth from them. I will show trust in order to build trust. When they arrive and I tell them they will be reporting to me, I lean into my **honesty**, **openness**, **transparency**, and **vulnerability** superpowers and also share that I am honored to be in this, my first leadership role, with them as my first direct reports. Then I invite them to help me establish our product management function, exhaling a deep sigh of relief when they accept.

An Extraordinary Opportunity

In early 2022 I attended (re)Discover Your Spark, an online weekend retreat created and facilitated by a local life coach, Dayna Del Val. I had known for a while that I wanted something more in my professional life, but I wasn't sure what that "more" was. I was hoping the retreat would help me figure it out, or at least point me in a new direction. I had no idea what signing up for that retreat would lead to! During the days that unfolded, we talked a lot about purpose, how we were made to be and do something extraordinary. This is where I met Jessica Buchanan; she was one of the other attendees in the retreat. I had no idea who Jessica was before this retreat, and during our first day she talked a bit about her kidnapping, but mostly she shared about the business ventures she was involved in, some of which she was questioning.

On our second day, we were tasked with writing our eulogies, and as we bravely took our turns sharing what we had written, it was impossible not to notice that Jessica was deeply moved. She kept wiping away tears, trying to catch them before they streamed down her face, and after one attendee read her very moving eulogy, Jessica asked to wait to take her turn so she could regain her composure. I wasn't expecting this reaction from her based on how calm, cool, and collected she had been prior to this. In fact, prior to this, I was feeling intimidated by her. But seeing such an honest and emotional reaction from her, I felt drawn to her. When she later described a project she was considering, an anthology, with chapters written by women who had gone through a desert of some kind, I thought, *I am going to buy that book!* and tucked the thought away.

After the retreat, I decided to use one of my Audible credits to order Jessica's book, *Impossible Odds*, and as I listened to it over the next few days, I couldn't believe I had been in the same retreat with this woman. I was in complete awe of how brave and strong she was after surviving such an ordeal, which made me even more interested in her anthology idea. I decided to follow her on LinkedIn so I could watch for updates. Every time I saw a post from her, as she worked to recruit contributing authors, I felt something inside me, a twinge, a nudge, prompting me to reach out to her. I ignored it, telling myself I didn't have a story even somewhat comparable to hers, but I decided to check out her website in spite of myself. As I took in the information about the anthology I couldn't ignore the repeated twinging. Finally, I gave in, and I reached out to her from our retreat email list, asking if we could meet. When she agreed I started making a list, jotting down in my phone's Notes app everything I could think of about what I thought might be a story. When I joined our Zoom call I could barely think, thankful for the notes I had jotted down, still unsure if I had anything worth writing. As I read through my bulleted list, tentatively sharing things I had gone through as a child that seemed like nothing compared to her story, Jessica was attentive. She listened. She occasionally asked a few questions. She even shared an experience from her own childhood. When I finished, she was silent for a moment, then she said in that voice I had heard during the retreat when she asked for more time to compose herself, "Ruth, thank you for trusting me with this. You definitely have a story." I let out the breath I hadn't realized I had been holding. She saw me. She heard me.

Jessica invited me during that call to join her anthology. It was an investment, so I asked for a few days to think about it, but I knew I wanted to say yes. I knew I would be in good hands with her, because I already felt like I knew her. She had been so honest, open, and vulnerable, showing me her true self, first during our retreat, then in her book, and again during our brief meeting.

I did decide to write a chapter in Jessica's first anthology, *Deserts to Mountaintops: Our Collective Journey to (re)Claiming Our Voice*. In my chapter, titled "Nothing Really Happened," I shared my story of child sexual abuse by an uncle who lived with my grandparents and later came to live with us. I grew up in constant fear of this uncle, trying to avoid him, but pressured by my parents to be polite to him. Another layer of my story is the environment I grew up in, surrounded by a perpetual state of mess, created by parents who were what we would now call hoarders.

Prior to my call with Jessica, I had shared only vague references of my child sexual abuse with a few people; I had never shared details. I was a little more open about growing up in a hoarder household, but again, I had never shared details. I decided to share my story because I wanted to let go of the secrets and shame I had carried for decades on my own. I wanted to spread awareness and bring hope to other survivors. And, because Jessica had leaned into her **honesty**, **openness**, and **vulnerability** superpowers, I trusted her. Sharing my story was terrifying, but it was also healing and empowering, and it allowed me to work with and get to know many real-life, super strong, wonder women.

Writing My Chapter

Once I made the decision to write a chapter in the anthology, one of my first steps was to meet with Jessica to discuss my story in more depth. This is when things got real. I found myself telling her details I had not told anyone, even Dale. Again, as I talked, Jessica was attentive, listening intently and occasionally asking questions. She helped me work through key points to include in my chapter, what piece of my story to begin my chapter with, and then it was my job to write it out. I had written short business articles previously, but nothing this personal or this long. Someone had given me a tip to get started when staring at a blank screen: just write; don't worry about editing, just write, even if it feels like garbage. So that's what I did. I poured everything out, spending my warm summer weekend days at our lake home staring into my laptop, frantically typing to get everything out of my head. As I wrote, memories I had kept locked away began to come back to me, bringing with them long buried feelings of being terrified, sad, lonely, and angry.

I felt pretty good about my first draft when I was finished. I asked Dale, our daughter Emma, and a close friend to read it before I submitted it to Jessica. Dale didn't say much after reading it, but he gave me a big, warm hug. Emma also gave me a hug and said softly into my ear, "It's good, Mom." I'm not sure they knew what else to do or say. It was a lot of new information for both of them to absorb. My friend had already read so many versions of my chapter by this point; she was my support person throughout the process.

I sat facing my laptop, took a deep breath, and anxiously clicked Share in Google Docs on my chapter, sharing it with Jessica, then followed up with an email to let her know it was ready for her review. I waited impatiently over the next few days, wondering what she would think and what she would say. The wait was excruciating. But when I saw her edits start to come into my email, one after another, that was so much worse than the waiting! There were so many edits and comments, and she kept repeating, "Show me! Don't tell me!" I didn't understand. I wanted to crawl back into bed, bury myself under the safety of the covers, and stay there. I didn't do that, but I did step away from my phone and my laptop for a while so I could breathe.

A few days later, when Jessica let me know she was done editing, I hesitantly opened the document to review the updates she had made. There were so many edits and comments. I thought about closing the document and my laptop and leaving the room, but I made myself read through them, telling myself these are helpful and valuable. As I read, fears like *What if this was a mistake?* and *What if I can't do this?* popped into my head in a repeating loop, but I kept reading until I reached the end. In her email letting me know she was done editing Jessica had suggested I read a memoir or two, and she gave me some recommendations. Before I started updating the document based on her edits and comments, I listened to one, and not very far in, I felt as if a light bulb had been switched on in my head. I got it! I understood what she meant by "Show me! Don't tell me!" Ruthie Lindsey, author of *There I Am: The Journey from Hopelessness to Healing*, took me back to what she had experienced, as she experienced it, using her words to vividly describe what she was seeing, hearing, smelling, tasting, and feeling. I had not done that. I had written my chapter at a very high level, as if I was someone reporting on an event, not as someone who had lived through a trauma.

My second draft was much more detailed. I tried to write as if I had gone back in time, to when I experienced my story, capturing the details of what I had seen, heard, smelled, tasted, and felt. This version was much harder for me to write, remembering details and re-experiencing feelings I really didn't want to remember or re-experience. But I wanted what Jessica wanted, to take the reader with me into my story. My five sisters and I were having a weekend get-together at our lake home the weekend before this draft was due. I worked diligently to make sure I had my draft ready ahead of time so I could enjoy spending the weekend with them. After I clicked Share on this version, I printed out a paper copy, hoping they would each want to read it. I had told a couple of them I was writing this chapter, but not all of them. As they arrived at various times throughout that Friday and Saturday, I asked them if they wanted to read my chapter. They all said yes. I sat nearby as each of them took turns reading it, trying to focus on the mystery game jigsaw puzzle we were working to solve together instead of staring at the sister holding the white printed pages with my secrets in their hands. I didn't know how they would react, with some of them having just learned I was writing this chapter, and I was sharing not just my secrets but our family's secrets. My terror dissolved as, one after another, they responded with hugs, support, and in some cases, shares of their own.

I knew I was on the right track when I saw "Yes!" scattered throughout Jessica's edits of this draft. I had to cut quite a bit from this version as it had grown lengthy with my added details. A lot of what was removed were sections that were intended to show my experience growing up wasn't entirely awful. We decided these sections, although interesting, could be removed without losing the main points of my chapter.

In my final one-on-one meeting for the anthology with Jessica, she asked me to read my chapter out loud to her. She wanted to see how long it took to read it, wanting each chapter to take about thirty minutes and knowing mine was still a bit long. As I read my chapter, which I had read aloud a few times the night before on my own, Jessica listened intently, noting in the document phrases or sections she felt we could remove. As I neared the end, I hit a section I had worked really hard on, one I was really proud of, and one I was hoping Jessica wouldn't ask me to cut or change. I started to choke up and we had to stop the timer. Jessica thought it was from me feeling the emotions of my past, but it was actually more about what I had accomplished, what she had helped me accomplish. I was so happy to be at this point, close to sharing my story with the world, hoping at least one person would read my story and feel less alone.

When I could, I started reading again. We had to stop a few more times, with Jessica patiently letting me pause, feel my feelings, then continue. After we wrapped up our call, I made the final edits we had discussed, let Jessica know I was done, and breathed a huge sigh of relief. My chapter was done!

The entire writing and editing process was an exercise in trust. I trusted Jessica to guide me through the process. She trusted me to listen to her advice, incorporate her feedback, and write a compelling story that people would want to read. When my first draft needed more show than tell, she provided that feedback, along with tips and resources for how to do it, leaning into her **honesty** and **openness** superpowers to help me "get it." I myself leaned into my **vulnerability** superpower, trusting Jessica and my early readers with my story, hoping they would respond with compassion and support, which they did.

Sharing My Chapter

Shortly after sending my email to Jessica, a new panic started to rise up in me as I realized the next step was to share my chapter with my peer review group. Jessica had grouped the twenty-three contributing authors into five peer review groups, with four to six authors in each group. I had met my co-authors on Zoom calls and I followed them all on Instagram, but I didn't know any of them well. The thought of sharing my chapter, something so personal and revealing, was terrifying to me. We were to share our chapters with our peer group, read each other's chapters, and thoughtfully and thoroughly provide each author with comments regarding three things: what we loved about their piece, what worked about their piece, what left us with questions or what questions we might still have about their piece. Jessica stressed to us that this was not an editing session, but a peer review feedback experience. I was very thankful for that.

My panic was unwarranted. My peer review group experience was wonderful. The women in my peer review group were warm, kind, thoughtful, and encouraging in their feedback. They each thanked me for sharing my story, assuring me that they believed it will help someone, further confirming my decision to join this project. One of my peer reviewers had written in her chapter about her own experience of child sexual abuse by her uncle. Two of my peer reviewers mentioned in their feedback that they or someone they knew had experienced abuse. One especially meaningful comment was that my writing was raw, open, and honest. As I read through each of their chapters, learning more about their own desert to mountaintop journey, I was drawn in, wanting to know more about them. The experience made me feel close to them, a bond I wasn't expecting and one that I can't imagine breaking.

During the writing process we were also actively promoting the anthology, primarily on Instagram but also on LinkedIn. Jessica had asked me early on in the project if I had an Instagram account, and if not, could I create one. I was on LinkedIn and had several connections, but I was not on any other social media platform. I knew nothing about Instagram, and this request intimidated me. I asked Emma to help me set up my account, and in the beginning I asked her so many questions about posts, stories, and reels, her eyes must have been tired from rolling back in her head, but she was an immense help. I shared more on Instagram, at least early on in the process, because I felt safer posting there, where I had only a few followers, mostly because of the anthology, where on LinkedIn, my connections knew me from my professional past. It was frightening to reveal such vulnerable pieces of myself online, but each time I did, it got easier.

One of our promotional tasks was to assemble a team of book ambassadors, people who would commit to prereading our chapter, buying the anthology on launch day, and submitting an Amazon review that same day. I was thankful for the predefined template we were provided for this, which made it easier to post on Instagram and LinkedIn, asking for people to join my team. I also messaged a few people through text and email. I didn't expect many responses, but I ended up with almost twenty people, a great team of supporters made up of close friends and family members. Stalwart Sage, who had moved on from NAGPS by this time, and two of my NAGPS colleagues were members of my team. I shared a bit about my story when I posted and messaged about joining my book ambassador team, but when it was time to actually send my chapter to my book ambassadors, my hands were shaking as I typed up the email and attached my chapter, knowing they were about to read details about me they might not be prepared for. I took a deep breath, leaned into my *vulnerability* superpower again, and hit Send. As their responses came back, sharing the reviews they planned to post on launch day, many also shared encouraging comments, and a few shared their own stories of child sexual abuse, again confirming for me that I was doing the right thing by telling my story. Every time I read one of their responses I felt like their arms were reaching through my laptop to give me a warm, supportive hug. The book ambassador process made me feel very connected to my team and gave me confidence going into our launch, knowing they had all read my story and would be supporting me on launch day.

Author Copies

We were given the opportunity to purchase author copies of the anthology at a reduced price prior to the book launch. A few weeks before the launch, we started to receive these copies, and we took turns sharing Instagram reels of us excitedly opening our boxes of books.

Jessica's books came first, and I loved her reel, narrating in a singsong voice as she showed the front cover, flipped through the pages somehow miraculously landing on my chapter where she said, "Ruth," then showed the back cover with our names, then the binding. I couldn't stop watching it! When my boxes came, I posted my own reel, with me opening a box in front of our Christmas tree, pulling out a book and finding my chapter, but Jessica's will always hold a special place in my heart.

Shortly after we had received our author copies, Jessica sent us an email, revealing that there was an issue with the copies we had received. She leaned into her **honesty**, **openness**, and **transparency** superpowers in this email, sharing her frustration as well as her gratefulness that the issue was caught prior to launch. She noted that author copies often do contain errors, but she also acknowledged that we had likely purchased these books to give out to our families, friends, and communities. She was right. I had already given out several copies to my family members, friends, and book ambassadors. She told us she had agonized over how to handle this with her team, wanting to honor our stories with integrity and transparency, and they had decided to replace each author's book order, covering the expense. She apologized, acknowledging we might have feelings of frustration and concern, and she offered to have a conversation with anyone who might want one. As always, she ended her email with encouragement, "Thank you always, for your commitment to *Deserts to Mountaintops*—I know your stories are going to help heal so many people. I can't wait to see it take flight!"

I was not upset, but rather amazed by her transparency, and I wasn't alone. I watched responses from my co-authors come in, and they were all positive and encouraging. I read words like *collaboration, empathy, understanding,* and *accountability* and decided to send Jessica a private message, "I can't imagine today's email was an easy one to send. I am so appreciative of your transparent and quick response, and I hope you are feeling that from everyone." What I witnessed was a perfect example of how to really trust your team. Leaning into her **openness**, **honesty**, and **transparency** superpowers allowed Jessica to build trust in a difficult situation rather than destroy it.

Following Jessica's lead, I reached out to those I had already given copies to, disclosing that the copies they had received contained errors but could be considered "limited edition." I offered to replace their copies with revised editions. To those I had planned to give copies to but hadn't yet, I offered a limited edition or a revised edition. Leaning into my own **honesty**, **openness**, and **transparency** superpowers was definitely the way to go, as not one person requested a replacement. Everyone wanted the limited edition. I tried not to influence their decision but perhaps was more persuasive than I realized when mentioning that the limited edition could be considered a collectible.

The Launch

I took our launch day off from work, knowing it would be a busy day. I woke up bright and early that morning to message my book ambassador team, reminding them to purchase their copy of the anthology and submit their review. Then I monitored the book on Amazon, reading through reviews and watching for reviews from my ambassador team to appear. The minute I saw one, or I received a message from a team member telling me they had submitted their review, I sent a thank you message, expressing my gratitude for their support. At the same time, I was reading and responding to exciting updates, encouragement, and congratulations from Jessica and my co-authors in our WhatsApp Anthology Sisters group chat, then sharing these updates with my book ambassador team. I also delivered a few books to members of my book ambassador team that morning and early afternoon. Later that afternoon, as things started to wind down, I drove to a local coffee shop that had agreed to let me have a small launch gathering to celebrate with my book ambassadors and family members who could make it. When I walked in, the first thing I noticed besides the glass counter holding assorted meats and cheeses was three of my sisters waiting for me. I walked over to their table, expecting to join them, and they pointed to a table in the corner, with a small table sign, "Reserved for Ruth." This was a fun surprise, having just requested use of the space during a typically quiet period of their day. I wasn't expecting a designated space. As I sat and celebrated with my small group of supporters that afternoon, I smiled and took in a deep breath, humbled and honored to be a part of the anthology and so happy I had trusted Jessica. It was an unbelievably fulfilling day.

The anthology did extremely well on launch day, hitting Best Seller in several categories on Amazon. We were encouraged to promote our book by reaching out to local bookstores and businesses to see if they would be interested in selling it. This was not natural for me, but I did reach out to a few, including the cider bar mentioned in the opening scene of this book. We were visiting the cider bar, located near our lake home, when I noticed a book displayed on a ledge along with a small sign about the author. I thought, *I should ask if they want to sell our book*—but when we ordered our ciders, I chickened out. As I sat sipping my drink, I kept telling myself I needed to do it and finally, I hesitantly stood up. Leaning into my **vulnerability** superpower, I stepped up to the counter and mentioned the book I had seen to one of the owners, asking if they would be interested in selling another book. She told me she was doing it as a favor for the local author and didn't have much space, but she agreed to take a look at the book after I told her I was also a local author. I ran out to my car and got one to show her, and when she stopped by our table, she said, "OK, tell me about this book." I described Jessica's story and how she wanted to help other women tell their stories, and I mentioned my story, showing her my chapter. She glanced through the book and said, "I'll take four to sell, and I want one for myself." I'm so glad I found the strength that day to walk up to the counter and ask her; that cider bar has been my best book seller! I also promoted our book by donating several copies to nonprofit organizations as silent auction items for their annual fundraising events.

Almost all of the contributing authors were able to meet in person at a launch party Jessica hosted a few days after the launch. The experience was exhilarating, overwhelming, and exhausting. Meeting Jessica and my co-authors in person was thrilling, and standing in line together signing books was an experience I will never forget. As I crawled into bed that night, my mind exhausted from talking with so many people and my fingers cramped from signing so many copies of our book, I still couldn't believe I was a published author who had shared my hard secrets with the world. Jessica brought together a group of women, many of whom had never met each other, and together we created something amazing. We recently had a catch-up Zoom call for those who could attend, and during the call, as we took turns updating everyone on what we are doing now, almost every one of us mentioned how we still feel so connected to and empowered by this group.

Sharing with My Team

I didn't mention the anthology project to the New Synergy Squad or to Ironmind as I worked on my chapter, but as launch day approached, I decided it was time to share. One week during our one-on-one meetings, after we had talked through their topics, I leaned into my *transparency* and *vulnerability* superpowers and told each of my team members about the book. My voice and hands were shaking as I told them about meeting Jessica, working on the project, and the content of my chapter. I wasn't sure how they would respond, but everyone was so supportive. They were very interested, asking questions to learn more about the process and my chapter. I answered their questions, leaning into my *openness* and *honesty* superpowers, and I offered each of them an early edition copy of the book, which they all eagerly accepted. They each let me know after reading my chapter that they really appreciated me sharing it with them. Organized Oracle was even able to help me celebrate our launch by attending our launch party with her fiancé, as she lived only an hour from the party location. Although I wasn't able to spend much time with her during the party, only greeting her briefly when they arrived and thanking her for coming and saying goodbye as they prepared to leave in the midst of our book signing extravaganza, I was so appreciative that she wanted to be there to celebrate with me and so glad I had decided to be transparent and vulnerable with my team.

The same week I shared with my team, I tried to share with Ironmind in our one-on-one meeting. I told him I had been working on the anthology, and before I could say more he interrupted me, saying he had seen my posts about my chapter on LinkedIn. I could tell he was uncomfortable with the topic and didn't want to talk about it, so I dropped it. We never discussed it again.

TRUST SUPERPOWERS

Superpower	Activation
Honesty	I lean into my ***honesty*** superpower by telling the truth and ensuring my words and actions are in alignment. I admit and take responsibility for mistakes and deliver honest feedback with tact and respect.
Openness	I embrace my ***openness*** superpower by sharing my thoughts and feelings to promote understanding. I seek deeper connections and encourage others to do the same by creating a safe, nonjudgmental space.
Transparency	I set clear expectations and communicate openly to lean into my ***transparency*** superpower. I like to ensure prompt sharing of relevant information to keep everyone informed and maintain consistency in communication to build trust and reliability.
Vulnerability	To embrace my ***vulnerability*** superpower, I openly share my challenges and my vulnerabilities, acknowledging my need for support and asking for help when needed. Additionally, I embrace discomfort and push beyond my comfort zone for personal growth.

TRUST WRAP-UP

American lawyer and politician Kirsten Gillibrand once said, "I find that when you open the door toward openness and transparency, a lot of people will follow you through." This rings true, especially in my experiences contributing to the anthology, making it a central theme of this chapter. By leaning into your superpowers of ***honesty***, ***openness***, *transparency*, and **vulnerability** to let your team know you, you will create an environment where everyone feels trusted.

TRUST REFLECTION

1. Which superpowers really stood out to you in this chapter?
2. Which of these superpowers are most natural for you?
3. Which of these superpowers are most challenging for you?
4. Which story or stories in this chapter did you most relate to?
5. Which story or stories did you least relate to?
6. Have you shared something personal with your team? What was their response?
7. What holds you back from opening up to your team?
8. What are some ways you can Trust: Let Your Team Know You?

TRUST

Story and illustration by Nathan Long

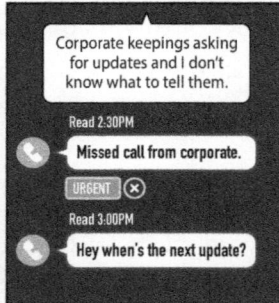

CHAPTER 4

Reinforce: Let Your Team Be Themselves

Reinforce, as defined by Dictionary.com, means:

- "to strengthen with some added piece, support, or material"

Recognizing Strengths

When Dale and I left Fargo for our big city adventure, I was fortunate to quickly find a job in the technology division of an accounting firm that provided consulting services to clients using GPS's software. My role consisted of remote and onsite consulting, answering client calls through our support line and helping clients implement and troubleshoot software at their offices. Both were overwhelming at first;

taking calls from clients I didn't know, unsure of what questions they might ask, and navigating through heavy urban traffic to reach clients' offices, as well as attempting to project an air of expertise despite rarely feeling like an expert, exhausted me.

I'll never forget one afternoon that had been particularly challenging. I had spent all afternoon at a client's office, wasting way too many of my client's checks attempting to get the alignment right for their first check run. I almost squealed in delight when I finally got all of the checks to print correctly and left the client's office flying as high as a helium-filled balloon. By the time I returned to our office the adrenaline had worn off and I started to feel the effects of my muscles being tense all afternoon as I watched check after check creep out of alignment. My shoulders were slumped as I walked through the doors, heading toward my desk. Completely exhausted, my head perked up when I saw a stack of papers on my desk. I knew what the stack was before I picked it up: printouts of client calls. After every client call we took, we logged what the call was about, along with the resolution, in a database. This was a helpful resource to reference when faced with a client issue we hadn't seen before, as often someone else had. Every week our manager reviewed the past week's calls, looking for good examples to review during our weekly team meeting. On the top of each of our stacks of calls to review was always a note, handwritten on our manager's personalized stationery. I picked up this week's note, which read, "Ruth, It makes me feel really good when I learn from reading these calls! I appreciate the way you handle these calls and your ability to resolve them in such a methodical manner. Keep up the good work!" My energy and spirit instantly lifted, as if my balloon self had just sucked in a lungful of helium. Finding a stack of papers topped by her personalized note recognizing my strengths was a highlight of my week; what a gift it was to leave my work day smiling! My manager was an expert at this, recognizing my strengths, highlighting clearly what I was doing well. When she heard from a client that they loved working with me because of my patient approach, she relayed that message to me, reinforcing that by listening and calmly asking questions, I reassured and calmed them, leading them down the pathway to trust me. She pointed out that my ability to reassure clients when they were panicking about an issue was a superpower that not everyone had, and that clients didn't care how long it took me to find a solution; they just needed to know I wouldn't give up until I had one. Hearing this from her meant a lot to me, because early on I had so much to learn. It often took me longer than others to get to a resolution, and I worried clients would get frustrated. She leaned into her **calmness**, **encouragement**, and **responsiveness** superpowers to recognize and encourage me to lean into my natural strengths instead of focusing on and trying to fix my weaknesses.

Several years later, I found myself in a different, smaller conference room at the insurance company, having recently transitioned from my role in the audit department to that of a project manager role. I was with two of my coworkers; one a relatively new project manager like me, and the other, a more experienced project manager, who had somewhat strongly suggested that he take on the role of becoming our mentor. Because we were thirsty for knowledge, we enthusiastically agreed to his plan. We were excited to learn as much as we could about project management! She and I sat at attention, side by side, while he took his position at the head of the room. Marker in hand, he was oblivious to the incessant screeching he was creating with his animated drawing of shapes and arrows across the whiteboard. We were with him, soaking in everything he said and drew, until he wrote CONTROL, in huge capital letters, on the whiteboard and asserted in our direction, "You need to want CONTROL. You will not succeed as project managers if you don't want CONTROL." I looked over at my coworker and saw confusion in her eyes that mirrored my own. I gathered my courage to ask for clarity, wanting to be sure I understood that what he thought control meant was what I thought control meant. Clearing my throat, I asked, "Do you mind elaborating on what you mean by CONTROL?" emulating his emphasis on the last word. He took a deep breath and slowly let it out, clearly trying to appear calm, but not doing a very good job. He continued, "You need to want control of everything about a project." He wrote the words "schedule, budget, people" on the board, saying the words aloud as he wrote them, then repeating each word as he underlined it. Then he said, "Your project team needs to know you are in control." I thought, *Okay, we might not be so far off,* understanding that time, cost, and resources are the key things that need to be managed in a project, but then he followed with, "Unless you work on being more commanding, you will struggle with your projects." My coworker and I looked at each other again, this time in matching feelings of disbelief. Commanding was not a quality either one of us held or wanted to develop! After several attempts to get him to acknowledge that we could be in control of a project without wanting to control people, by using skills such as collaboration, we gave up, realizing we would never convince him.

As we filed out of the conference room, still shell-shocked by what we had just witnessed, my colleague and I had what would be the first of several private conversations about this. We were in agreement that we were not willing (or able) to change our personalities to fit his definition of a successful project manager. We were determined to be collaborative project managers, working alongside our project teams to control *outcomes,* not *people.* We chose to lean into our superpowers of **courage,** *integrity*, and *respect*, holding firmly to our belief that collaborating would triumph over the act of controlling. We have stayed in touch (she was one of my book ambassadors for the anthology), and we have both been successful in our project management careers. Recently, a former project sponsor, one I worked with after this, reinforced that we were justified in sticking with our approach when he shared in a conversation, "BTW, you were the best PM I had the pleasure of working with."

A few years after our CONTROL incident, I was sitting across the desk from one of my project sponsors at the hospitality company, the one who had gone all in on implementing Good News with me. I had followed him to his office after our weekly project team meeting to discuss an issue we had just learned about from our vendor. My heels were up to no good, bouncing up and down even though I kept willing them to stop, as I sat waiting for him to redock his laptop, settle in, and give me his full attention. When he finally looked up at me from across his desk, I was expecting to see concern. Instead, he said, rather bluntly, "Ruth, you remind me of a duck." I tilted my head, giving him a perplexed look, thinking, but not voicing, *Is reminding you of a duck a good thing or a bad thing?* As if on cue, he smirked, letting me know it was a good thing, then proceeded to describe how a duck will paddle madly underneath the surface of the water to make itself move, but above the surface, what we see is its calm and seemingly relaxed body propelling forward, as if this movement takes absolutely no effort. He was giving me a huge compliment, albeit, in a roundabout way, by sharing that he respected my ability to handle issues with grace and composure, even though he understood, at least at times, I had to be panicking inside. He leaned into his superpowers of *encouragement* and *respect*, recognized my strength of projecting calm even when I didn't feel it, and without me telling them to, my feet stopped their bouncing.

During this same period of time I retook the CliftonStrengths assessment, curious to see if, or how much, my results would differ from when I took it the first time. As I read through my new CliftonStrengths report I was fascinated with how well it reflected my strengths, and me:

- Individualization: You are intrigued with the unique qualities of each person. You have a gift for figuring out how different people can work together productively.
- Empathy: You can sense other people's feelings by imagining yourself in others' lives or situations.
- Developer: You recognize and cultivate the potential in others. You spot the signs of each small improvement and derive satisfaction from evidence of progress.
- Learner: You have a great desire to learn and want to continuously improve. The process of learning, rather than the outcome, excites you.
- Relator: You enjoy close relationships with others. You find deep satisfaction in working hard with friends to achieve a goal.

The report also showed that I lead with Relationship Building themes, which help me build strong relationships that hold a team together.

It took me many years and many different roles to recognize and lean into my own strengths instead of trying to emulate strengths I saw in others. A few of my managers tried to change me into someone they thought I should be instead of recognizing and helping me embrace my natural abilities, making me feel like I was wearing the still-shrunken Wasp suit, unable to move and unable to breathe. One example was frequently being told I am too quiet. If you recall, according to my MBTI assessment, I am introverted. Whenever someone chided me for being too quiet, it felt like I was being reprimanded for being too human. I tried to be "less quiet" by trying to talk more in group settings, make quicker decisions, and act more confident than I felt, but I came to recognize and appreciate that quiet strength is a superpower! Harry Lakin, founder and CEO of Hire Capacity, posted a LinkedIn article recently that reinforced this idea for me. It was titled, "Quiet Strength: Unleashing the Power of Introverted Leadership," in which he stated, "Introverts possess a wealth of characteristics that distinguish them in leadership roles. Their ability to listen actively and process information deeply sets them apart in decision-making processes. Introverted leaders are known for carefully weighing options, considering multiple perspectives, and making well-informed choices. This thoughtful approach not only leads to sound decisions but also fosters an environment where team members feel heard and valued." As I read his article on a chilly February morning, I could hardly get my coffee down over the lump in my throat at reading such truth. I couldn't have agreed more with what I was reading! In the wise words of Michaela Chung, author of *The Irresistible Introvert: Harness the Power of Quiet Charisma in a Loud World* and *The Year of the Introvert: A Journal of Daily Inspiration for the Inwardly Inclined*, "Don't underestimate me because I'm quiet. I know more than I say, think more than I speak, and observe more than you know."

My mission in leading the Powerhouse Pair, Tenacious Triad, Synergy Squad, and New Synergy Squad was to recognize the individual strengths of each of my team members, not try to change them into someone else. I wanted them to feel like they were proudly sporting their own custom designed, perfectly fitted super suits that would elevate their strengths, like the ones Edna Mode designed for The Incredibles. Recognizing and leaning into my strengths ultimately led me to helping others recognize and lean into their own strengths, including writing this book, to help others lean into their superpowers!

Sharing Decisions

When I started working with the Powerhouse Pair, I had a big decision to make: Who will own our existing products and who will own the new product we are building? During their first several weeks, we spent time sequestered in a conference room, shifting our gaze between our laptops and the wall in front of us as we took turns sharing our screens and our knowledge. As we learned together, it became evident to me who should own which product, but I wanted this to be a joint decision. One afternoon I asked them what they were thinking, and to my relief, we all agreed that Stalwart Sage would own our existing products and Teamwork Titan would own the new product we were building. By inviting them to share in the decision, I had leaned into my *attentiveness*, *respect*, and *responsiveness* superpowers, showing them I recognized their individual strengths while respecting their input.

Hiring was another key decision I shared with my team members. As our team expanded and morphed from the Powerhouse Pair to the New Synergy Squad, I sought my team members' input in each hiring decision. Stalwart Sage and Teamwork Titan were fully behind asking Positivity Paladin to join our team after his internship. Organized Oracle and Boomerang Brainiac were both internal candidates, unanimously welcomed as brilliant additions to our team. I invited Organized Oracle to participate in interviews when we hired Counselor QuickStudy, and we both agreed she was the perfect choice. By leaning into my *respect* and *responsiveness* superpowers and involving my team in hiring decisions, I demonstrated that I not only recognized and supported their knowledge and expertise, I valued their insight into who would be a good fit for our team. I appreciated having their support and input as we expanded, knowing these decisions would impact everyone.

Focusing on the Positive

I forced myself to take a break from the spreadsheet I was studying to check my email, and the second I saw it my entire body froze. My new manager had told me she did quarterly assessments, but that didn't help me prepare for the wave of cold I felt wash over me when I saw the innocently titled but fear-inducing email, Employee Quarterly Assessment. I shivered, my blood chilled as if someone had injected me with liquid nitrogen.

This wasn't the first time I had this reaction to a pending review. For years I had experienced some level of panic any time the words *performance review* were mentioned in my presence. In an attempt to understand why, I brainstormed potential reasons inside my head: One, I am a perfectionist and a people pleaser—receiving feedback that I am not "perfect" makes me feel like I have let someone down, and when delivered without support, it feels isolating; two, bragging about myself, which I feel pressured to do when asked to complete a self-assessment, a common element of a performance review, feels unnatural to me; three, self-assessments, especially those that require self-ratings, feel like a mind-reading exercise—I don't want to underestimate myself or worse yet, overestimate myself; four, I have frequently been told I am too quiet or need to project more confidence, as if I am Jennifer Walters and can morph myself into She-Hulk, instantly becoming taller, louder, and more domineering.

Thankfully this quarterly assessment didn't include a self-assessment, so I didn't need to brag or try to guess my manager's ratings. I just had to show up and get through the review. I was grateful she had scheduled it in the morning and not for later in the afternoon. Still, I couldn't keep my eyes on my work, but rather kept glancing at the clock in the lower right corner of my computer screen, anxiously waiting for the time to pass. A few minutes before the meeting, I sprinted over to the restroom and quickly emptied my bladder. No one wants to realize they need to run to the ladies' room in the middle of an evaluation! Then grabbing my laptop, just in case I needed it, I made my way over to her office. As I closed the door behind me, my manager's eyes shifted from her computer screen up to me and she smiled, gesturing with her hands for me to take a seat across the desk from her. Then she handed me a copy of my review. I glanced through it quickly before she started, noticing the many checkmarks beneath Meets Expectations and a few under Exceeds Expectations. My muscles started to relax realizing this wasn't going to be the disaster I feared; then she began. As we read through the review document together, she summarized her comments, looking up frequently to smile at me, assuring me repeatedly about what a great job I was doing and how happy she was that I was there. She focused on things I was doing well, noting responsibilities from my job description that I was well aware of and that we had discussed in previous conversations. When we got to the last page, I followed along with what she had written as she summarized, and a smile spread across my face as she read her final comment, "You are doing a great job so far! I really appreciate your willingness to jump in and get things done." I left her office a few minutes later smiling so widely my cheeks hurt and doing my very best to walk without skipping. She had embraced her superpowers of *attentiveness*, *encouragement*, and *respect*, delivering a review that left me feeling relieved, supported, proud of my accomplishments, and determined to achieve even more.

In this review she didn't suggest any improvements, but in subsequent reviews she did, always accompanying them with tips for how I could improve, all while offering her support. Our manager at the accounting firm also did this. For example, she suggested I might feel more confident with our clients if I increased my accounting expertise by taking some classes, leading me to seek out my MBA program. Then she fully supported me by writing a recommendation letter for my application, celebrating my acceptance, and promptly approving my tuition reimbursement requests. Our manager at the hospitality company did something similar, suggesting I might feel more confident leading meetings if I increased my public speaking skills, leading me to seek out the Dale Carnegie Course. Then she fully supported me emotionally and financially as I went through the program, including attending my final session where we celebrated our graduation. I'll never forget her telling me, "I have learned so much from you as you have gone through this course. I have been thinking about it, and I'm going to recommend that others on our team attend." What a compliment and boost to my confidence! These managers leaned into their ***attentiveness***, ***encouragement***, and ***respect*** superpowers, delivering suggestions for improvement in a positive, nonthreatening way, along with tips for how to improve and offering their support, making me feel motivated to implement their suggestions.

About two years after that first quarterly assessment with my manager, I was sitting at my same desk, studying a different spreadsheet, when I again decided to take a break and check my email. My breath caught in my throat. There it was, an email announcing our annual performance review process. My fingers shook as I moved my mouse across the screen to click on the email and open it, carefully reading through its contents:

- All performance reviews need to be completed within one month
  - Employees have two weeks to complete and submit their self-assessment to their managers

- Managers have one month to complete their employees' performance reviews, including meeting with each employee to go over their review
  · Peer feedback is encouraged but not required

The coldness in my blood had returned the minute I saw the email, this time multiplied. Not only would this be my first annual performance review with Ironmind, it would be my first time delivering performance reviews to my team.

In our next one-on-one meetings I reviewed the email with Stalwart Sage and Teamwork Titan, asking if they had any questions or concerns. "If you are okay with it, I would like to seek feedback from the people you work most closely with," I said to each of them, and they both agreed. After their one-on-one meetings, I sent emails to their peers, asking three questions: What they should keep doing, what they should start doing, and what they should stop doing. I also asked them to refrain from sharing with me anything they hadn't already shared directly with my team members. I didn't want to surprise my team members with feedback they were hearing for the first time in a review, reflecting my belief that recognition and constructive feedback should be given frequently and timely, not just once a year.

As feedback from their peers flowed in, I reviewed and considered it, incorporating what was relevant and valuable. I captured the full details in a separate document, planning to share it with them, but not wanting it to be included in their official review, in case they disagreed with something that was said. When I received their self-assessments, I added my feedback, pulling accomplishments from the Good News/ Best Professional/Best Personal and Status Updates sections of our team meeting notes. If I shared a suggestion for improvement, I also included tips for how to improve, as well as offering my support.

On review day, I met with each of them, handed them a copy of their review, and told them they could count on two things from me: One, I would always focus on the positive, and two, they should never be surprised by my feedback. I watched an overwhelming feeling of relief come over them as I explained this to each of them. Apparently I am not the only one who dreads performance reviews. I realized I should have communicated this message much earlier and made a mental note to do that in the future with any new members we added to our team. I wanted to avoid being the cause of anyone else feeling that dread. I then shared their peer feedback, and they both thanked me for not including it in the official review, because, as I had suspected, there was some feedback they did not fully agree with. By leaning into my **attentiveness**, **courage**, **integrity**, **respect**, and **responsiveness** superpowers, focusing on the positive and not surprising them, my hope was that they had a positive review experience with me and felt supported, proud of what they had accomplished, and motivated to continue their great work.

Although I completed and submitted my self-assessment to Ironmind on time, he never acknowledged it, and I never had a review that year, or the next.

Eventually, annual performance reviews became mandatory for everyone, and for the past two years, I have had one with Ironmind. For more than two years he has taken every opportunity, including these review meetings, to remind me that we need to release our new product. I don't need a reminder. I am well aware that we need to release this product as soon as possible. What I do need is his support, which I have pretty much given up on receiving after countless futile attempts to advocate for what my team needs. I lead the team who defines what functionality we want in our products and why we want it; the development team figures out how to build it and builds it, and my team is way ahead of the development team. We need the development team to build faster; we know we can keep up. This means we need more developers, but Ironmind does not want to hear this. He wants a miracle, some way to quickly replace a product that took decades to develop using our existing, miniscule team of developers.

I feel like I am in the movie *Doctor Strange*, where Doctor Strange uses the Time Stone to trap himself and Dormammu, the ruler of the Dark Dimension, a parallel universe of endless torment and hunger, in a time loop until Dormammu agrees to leave Earth with his Zealots and never return. I am trapped with Ironmind in what seems like an endless loop, having the same conversation over and over again. Ironmind holds me accountable for getting the new product out, but he provides no support in resolving the main issue preventing this from happening, the speed of our development team. I do not lead the development team. That team is led by Ironmind's buddy, who reinforces Ironmind's delusion that we can miraculously speed up development with the small team we have, but produces no evidence to prove this is possible. Let's call him Shadowwit, the one who follows without question. You will see him again too.

Knowing this will come up again in this year's annual performance review, I proactively add a response to the Impediments section of my self-assessment, answering the question "What help do you need to improve your work or accomplish your goals?" with "My team and I are limited in how fast we can enhance existing products and build new products by how fast the development team can implement. We consistently move work we would like to accomplish in a sprint to a future sprint based on team velocity." My optimistic, irrational self thinks, *Maybe this will convince him we need additional development resources to move faster.*

A few weeks later, as I log on to my virtual performance review meeting, my mind is racing, dreading the meeting and frantically wanting it to be over as quickly as possible. Things go well at first, with him telling me I am doing a good job managing my team. When we get to the Impediments section, I can't believe it when he says, "I agree with your assessment," but I know better than to get excited. I have been tricked into thinking he has heard me too many times before. I lean in closer to the screen as he proceeds, confirming my hesitation, "But we need to have a stronger vision of the product and what we want it to do." There it is. It's my fault. I slouch back in my chair, realizing my final plea for help was unheard, or more likely, ignored. This will forever be my issue to resolve, not Shadowwit's, and without Ironmind's support. As he wraps up our call, he tries to end on a positive note, reading from his final comments, "I think Ruth is doing a good job managing her team," and ending with, "I am grateful to have Ruth and her leadership on the team." Two months later I was laid off.

During my last two years at the company, team members were requested to complete an annual employee survey. Both years I received a summary report showing stats for my team. The first year my report showed performance scores of 93.8 for Appreciation and 100 percent for Respect, Supervisory Support, and Work-Life Balance. The second year my report showed performance scores of 100 percent for all of these categories. I was ecstatic to see these results in areas I prioritized with my team. When I met with Ironmind about them, I waited to hear him commend me for my high results. Instead I heard, in his by-then too familiar critical tone, "Why do you think your team's Work/Life Balance score is higher than the company's overall Work/Life Balance score?" Instead of receiving support and recognition for my dedication to my team, I felt scolded. He could just as well have said, "You are way too lenient with your team," because that is exactly what he meant.

Leading by Example

During our first several months together as a new product management team, the Powerhouse Pair and I spent many days returning to that same conference room, not only learning together but working to define our product management processes, tools, and templates. In addition to this work, I knew there was a daunting task looming over us, our gargantuan list of product enhancement requests from clients that needed to be reviewed and prioritized, deciding which ones we would address in our existing products and which ones could wait to be addressed in the new product we were building. After deciding product ownership, I could have delegated this task to Stalwart Sage and Teamwork Titan, trusting in their abilities and stepping away, but that didn't feel right to me. It wasn't that I didn't trust them; I absolutely did. I just knew it was an overwhelming task, and I wanted them to know they had my full support. So I leaned into my *attentiveness*, *integrity*, *patience*, *respect*, and *responsiveness* superpowers, rolled up my sleeves, and joined them, showing I was willing to dive in to help with hard work. As our team grew, I continued to offer my support in this way, never wanting anyone to feel alone and overwhelmed with a daunting task when I could help.

One Tuesday I was having a focus issue, thinking about our upcoming trip to San Diego. Our family had gone there several years before, and every time we talked about it afterward we referred to it as our favorite trip ever. This particular trip is where I learned I could run without absolutely hating it, the trick was listening to an interesting story. I would often remember taking in the gorgeous ocean view along the boardwalk and basking in the warm sunshine on my skin as I went through chapter after chapter of *The Hunger Games*. As my mind became immersed in Katniss's horrific world, the pain in my feet, legs, and lungs seemed to disappear, and the time and miles passed quickly. I had found my trick to running! I snapped back to the present to join my virtual one-on-one meeting with Teamwork Titan, and when we were done talking through her topics, I reminded her, "Remember, I'm on vacation next week. I can't wait!" She smiled and said, "Yay! I'm so happy for you!" and I could tell she genuinely meant it. We talked for a few minutes longer, with me sharing our plans for a kayak and snorkel tour and a whale and dolphin watching adventure, and then I said, as I had to each of my other team members earlier in the day, "I am planning to monitor emails, so if you need anything while I'm out, email me, and I will see it." She nodded and thanked me, but then, struck by a sudden thought, she looked intently into my eyes, "Wait! Is that what you expect of me when I go on vacation?" I'm pretty sure my face turned beet red or at least bright pink, because it was suddenly very hot! "No!" I blurted out, immediately realizing my mistake. I thought I had been doing a good thing, leaning into my *responsiveness* superpower, by telling my team I would check in while on vacation, but instead I was potentially setting up a dangerous expectation that they do the same. I meekly thanked Teamwork Titan for reminding me of the importance of leading by example, and after she left our meeting I immediately messaged my team, "Hi everyone! I have decided I will NOT be checking emails next week. I'm going to focus on enjoying my vacation." I then shared that Teamwork Titan had helped me realize my mistake, and shared my phone number, saying they could reach out if they needed me. A flurry of messages came back, thanking me and telling me to enjoy my vacation. This was my message from then on, whenever I took time off, and whenever my team members took time off, I encouraged them to check out, not check in. I hope they knew I meant it, having leaned into my ***attentiveness***, ***respect***, and ***responsiveness*** superpowers to lead by example.

About two years after our second awesome San Diego trip, NAGPS shifted from requiring annual performance reviews to requiring quarterly reviews. This meant every quarter, each employee was to complete and submit a self-assessment, to which their manager would respond, adding their own comments, followed by a meeting to discuss the review. I encouraged my team members to be brief in their self-assessments, knowing they had busy schedules, but I also let them know I enjoyed reading, responding to, and meeting with them to discuss their accomplishments, impediments, and what they had learned over the past quarter. Apparently following this process was too much for Ironmind, because he never responded to any of my quarterly self-assessments. The careful work I put into them was left untouched and unacknowledged. I couldn't imagine ignoring my team members' work—their time was important, why wasn't mine?

After several quarters of watching my stack of previously completed but ignored self-assessments build, one on top of another, clogging up our HR system, with a new to-be-completed request appearing every quarter at the top, I had had enough. I reached out to HR, asking to meet. When I joined the virtual meeting, I said, "I have consistently followed our quarterly review process, even though it at times feels like too much." She thanked me for following the process, noting that a few managers were never meeting with their team members, and this was meant to encourage more interaction. I thought but did not say, "So instead of directly dealing with that issue, we instead ask team members who are already overworked to do more work?" Instead, I said, "I have quarters of unacknowledged self-assessments stacked up. It doesn't feel good to be asked to do another self-assessment knowing it will not be read or acknowledged." She listened and empathized with me, then she said she would bring my concern to her manager and let me know what their next step would be. As we hung up, I felt better having voiced my concern but also worried I had made a mistake.

She messaged me a few days later, "I met with Ironmind, and I brought up your concern, and he told me even though the self-assessments aren't appearing as acknowledged in the system, they were all discussed. He also told me to tell you if you have further questions or concerns you should bring them directly to him." My body froze as my eyes stared at the screen and her message. What?! First, I wasn't expecting her to talk with him without letting me know (Ironmind was *not* her manager). Second, we had *never* discussed them; he had outright lied to her! Third, why was she sending me a message instead of talking with me? My feelings sprang back and forth between terrified and furious, my fingertips frozen on my keyboard for minutes, trying to come up with a response that would adequately communicate my reaction. Finally, I typed simply, "Thanks," my fingers stabbing the keys in hopes of conveying my frustration. I dropped my concern and never brought up another one again.

———

For more than two years, Ironmind stressed the importance of embracing diversity, equity, and inclusion (DEI), bringing DEI up frequently during all company meetings and encouraging us in leadership team meetings to consider DEI when hiring. In my second to last annual review with Ironmind he noted, "I think every leader in our business has to focus on understanding our commitment to DEI, and this will include more learning for our team." We had one training focused on DEI that year, a recording we were all required to watch, after which we were given a short quiz we needed to pass. In my last annual review with Ironmind he noted that he wanted every manager to be able to articulate what the company was doing to embrace DEI, listing a formalized policy, working with an external DEI consultant, and establishing a team-member-led DEI committee. Shortly after this, we acquired another company and Ironmind announced the new C-suite. The four most senior executives in this newly merged organization were all white, and all male. I was devastated, imagining how every team member who was not a white male felt at that moment. *Actions speak louder than words!* my inner voice chanted on repeat. My fingers found my keyboard and typed up several versions of this message to HR, but each time I stopped before I hit Send, backspacing to erase the words, knowing from experience it would get me nowhere, except possibly in trouble. A few weeks later, two of my team members and I were laid off. Two of us were female, while our male counterparts were retained.

Making Things Easier

One morning, long before Google Maps, I was in my office at the accounting firm, packing up to drive to a client's office, when our more senior consultant stopped in. She was carrying a piece of printer paper, which she put on my desk. Then she started drawing on it. She drew a small dot and labeled it "Our office," then she drew another small dot and labeled it "Client's office." She then proceeded to explain and draw how to get from our office to the client's office and how to get back. She knew I had come from a smaller city and wasn't used to driving in the Twin Cities metropolis, and she didn't want me to get lost. This was likely the result of me sharing how I had driven almost the entire Twin Cities Beltway, the huge loop formed by Interstates 494 and 694 around Minneapolis and Saint Paul, on my way back from a client's office because I had gotten on the loop going the wrong way and was afraid if I got off to turn around I might not find my way back on. Instead, I followed the loop, knowing I'd eventually get to where I needed to be.

When I got safely back to our office, I stopped by her desk to thank her. She smiled and said she was glad to help, then suggested I purchase a King's Twin Cities Metro Street Atlas, a spiral bound book of maps of the Twin Cities, to help me navigate the area. I took her sage advice, and used this book the entire time we lived there and for years after when we would return for a visit. Whether or not it was pity from my pathetic story that drove her or she just wanted to help me be successful, she leaned into her **attentiveness**, **calmness**, **patience**, **respect**, and **responsiveness** superpowers to make things easier for me, and she did it in a way that made me feel supported, not judged. It's been many years since that interaction, and I still remember how supported she made me feel.

Several years after moving back to Fargo, I was once again a beneficiary of someone making things easier for me. In my first IT auditor role, my manager contracted with Deloitte & Touche LLP to provide an experienced IT auditor to accompany me on my first audit. We sat side by side on the company plane on our way to the operating company, me watching him intently as he created an audit plan for us to follow. While I watched him fill in the spreadsheet on his laptop, he explained each audit step and how we would test it. When we got to the client's location, he led the audit, and I shadowed him, taking careful notes. On the plane ride home, we again sat side by side as he created an audit report, summarizing what we had found. I again watched and listened, as he carefully explained each audit finding and his recommendation for how the operating company could address it. At the end of this audit, I had an example audit plan, detailed notes, and an example audit report to use as starting points for audits at our other operating companies. Our manager wanted me to succeed but knew the IT auditor role would be a lot to take on. IT audit was a relatively new field, and she knew she didn't have the expertise to assist me as much as an expert in IT audit would. This shadowing experience provided me with templates and notes, but it also provided me with confidence I would not have gained as quickly if I had had to figure things out on my own. She leaned into her *attentiveness*, *respect*, and *responsiveness* superpowers and made things easier for me.

An opportunity to make things easier for my team arose when we were unexpectedly uprooted from our existing office space to a less than desirable space with very little notice and even less consideration. One morning I walked toward my cubicle, located on the second floor of our office building, back in a sheltered corner along a wall of windows I shared with Stalwart Sage and Teamwork Titan. From a distance I saw someone kneeling on the floor outside my cubicle. When I got closer I could see he was holding a tape measure, with the long metal end protruding into my cubicle. He was measuring our space! I asked him what he was doing, and he said he was measuring for the new offices we were putting in. My heart leapt, thinking, *Am I getting an office, finally?* and then Ironmind appeared. "Oh, I had planned to tell you this earlier, but I need to relocate you and your team somewhere else because we need to build offices for the additional sales team members we are hiring." As I watched the area continue to be measured, my heart sank. Not only was I not getting an office, I was losing a prime space that almost felt like an office, and so were Stalwart Sage and Teamwork Titan. We sat in a row along the windows, sheltered from distractions from three sides. Positivity Paladin was less fortunate. He sat out in the open, near the men's bathroom, overlooking our lobby. I asked Ironmind where we would be moving. He looked at me blankly, admitting he didn't have an answer for me.

Later, we found out we would be moving to a space near where Positivity Paladin was currently sitting, in the middle of the second floor, while the development team took over a space further back, with much more privacy. Before our move, we met several times as a team, to brainstorm how to arrange our desks to best fit our needs. We finally settled on a plan that we all liked, but it left us exposed on two sides. I wanted to provide us with more privacy, to lessen potential distractions, so I leaned into my *attentiveness*, *respect*, and *responsiveness* superpowers and looked into a solution. I explained the situation to my manager (not Ironmind at the time, a temporary, welcome reprieve who worked in a different office), and requested permission to order some privacy screens from Amazon. With his approval and a budget, I consulted with my team, and we selected screens together, simple bamboo with shelves on both sides, that we all agreed would look nice with our desk walls. By putting these screens along the outsides of our four desks, we could form an enclosed space for our team, giving each of us privacy on three sides. I was ecstatic to have this solution and make this move easier for all of us.

When our privacy screens arrived, Positivity Paladin helped me haul the big boxes upstairs. After he and I finished pulling the screens from their wrapping, we got busy assembling and setting them up in the pattern we had discussed. I was so busy arranging our new office footprint, I didn't notice when Ironmind materialized, seemingly out of nowhere. I looked up from gathering stray styrofoam sheets that had fluttered from the boxes to see him standing by my desk, his arms folded across his chest, a furrowed brow pasted across his face. "WHAT is happening here?" he bellowed loud enough I was sure nearby office mates were peeking around corners and over cubicle walls in curiosity. I nervously explained that after obtaining approval from my manager, and a budget, we had ordered privacy screens to help us feel less exposed in this wide open area that we had been relegated to. His brow furrowed even deeper into his stern face as he surveyed the bamboo material. "Well, I wish you would have consulted me first. I would have found privacy walls that would have looked better." I wanted to say, "Why didn't you offer this when you decided to relocate us?" but instead, I stayed silent. I watched Positivity Paladin's posture change. His body seemed to shrink as his shoulders slouched forward and his head bowed; our prior excitement had been zapped by Ironmind's callousness. After Ironmind returned to his private office suite, which was in direct view of us, I encouraged Positivity Paladin to help me continue setting up our screens, not wanting Ironmind's critical assessment to permanently damage our excitement.

When we finished our assembly, setup, and cleanup, I took a stroll around our space, admiring our creativity and resourcefulness. I was thankful for the shelter these simple screens would provide my team, not only from distractions but also from Ironmind's scrutiny as he sauntered past our area. I ordered several small wooden signs to display on the outside shelves of my privacy screen, with motivational sayings such as, "If you can be anything, be kind," "Today is a good day for a great day," "All things are possible," and "You are amazing. Remember that." Several months later we all relocated to our homes due to COVID-19 restrictions, and when, about a year later, we were offered the choice to return to the office or remain at home, my team members and I unanimously voted to remain at home. Ironmind told me he was surprised when he saw my vote; he thought I would want to return to the office. This baffled me because he had never attempted to make the office seem welcoming to me or to my team. The privacy screens had helped, but we were more than happy to give them up for the privacy and shelter our own home offices provided, away from him.

REINFORCE SUPERPOWERS

Superpower	Activation
Attentiveness	I lean into my **attentiveness** superpower by giving my full attention to the speaker, concentrating not only on their words but also on their body language and tone of voice. Additionally, I minimize distractions and stay mentally and emotionally present during interactions.
Calmness	To embrace my **calmness** superpower, I take deep breaths to maintain my composure and reduce stress. I find it helpful to respond thoughtfully rather than react impulsively, and to take time to consider a situation from multiple angles.
Courage	I lean into my **courage** superpower by envisioning the best possible outcome and taking action despite fear. I like to embrace vulnerability as a strength, being open about fears and insecurities while fostering authenticity in myself and others.
Encouragement	To lean into my **encouragement** superpower, I use my words and actions to demonstrate my belief in others' abilities and potential. I like to focus on effort and progress, celebrating small victories and acknowledging improvements, to provide motivation and momentum for further growth.

Superpower	Activation
Integrity	I lean into my *integrity* superpower by communicating openly and honestly, fostering trust and transparency. I admit mistakes and take responsibility, and I prioritize following company policies and leading by example.
Patience	I take deep breaths to calm my mind and maintain my composure to lean into my *patience* superpower. I like to listen attentively and stay objective, avoiding impulsive reactions and judgments based on emotions. I find it helpful to allow time for thoughtful consideration and avoid distractions.
Respect	I embrace my *respect* superpower by focusing on being polite and courteous in my interactions. I allow people to express themselves without interrupting them, to let them know that I value their thoughts and opinions. Most importantly, I avoid criticizing, judging, shaming, and humiliating anyone.
Responsiveness	I find that setting clear and realistic expectations helps me lean into my *responsiveness* superpower. I like to acknowledge messages promptly and follow up consistently, and I prioritize communicating proactively to keep people informed.

REINFORCE WRAP-UP

As American essayist, lecturer, and poet Ralph Waldo Emerson wisely stated, "To be yourself in a world that is constantly trying to make you something else is the greatest accomplishment." This quote exemplifies the theme of this chapter. By leaning into your superpowers of *attentiveness*, *calmness*, *courage*, *encouragement*, *integrity*, *patience*, *respect*, and *responsiveness* to let your team be themselves, you will create an environment where everyone feels supported.

REINFORCE REFLECTION

1. Which superpowers really stood out to you in this chapter?
2. Which of these superpowers are most natural for you?
3. Which of these superpowers are most challenging for you?
4. Which story or stories in this chapter did you most relate to?
5. Which story or stories did you least relate to?
6. How do you approach performance reviews with your team? Do you focus on their strengths or their weaknesses? How is that working for you (and for them)?
7. What are some ways you could make or have made things easier for your team?
8. What are some ways you can Reinforce: Let Your Team Be Themselves?

CHAPTER 5

Optimize: Let Your Team Shine

Optimize, as defined by Dictionary.com, means:

- "to make as effective, perfect, or useful as possible"
- "to make the best of"

Opportunities to Contribute

Back at GPS, many years before our CONTROL incident at the insurance company, I found myself sitting in a different conference room, equally as small, surrounded by a team of developers, designers, and testers. Our lead developer was standing in front of a whiteboard that spanned three of the four walls of the room, holding a similar marker but creating a much less intense screeching noise as he moved it across the shiny white surface. We were brainstorming a huge new feature, discussing how to build an Accounts Payable Historical Aged Trial Balance. If we did this correctly, it would be a brilliant addition to our software, a report that could look back at a previous month and tell someone what they owed their vendors at that time, as if they had traveled back to that month like they were Barry Allen, aka The Flash, using the Cosmic Treadmill.

Enthralled with the activity going on around me, I could feel the energy radiating from every person in the room. This was my first brainstorming experience, and I was loving it! Ideas surged in from every direction, sparking conversation with electric energy like Thor's lightning, one after another from meeting attendees gathered in the room, spurred by questions from our lead developer. He did his best to capture the ideas as quickly as they came, ensuring not one was lost or forgotten. Sometimes he asked clarifying questions, and often, he added his own thoughts, but with every suggestion, he nodded his head vigorously in agreement, as if every person's idea was the best one yet. At first I sat quietly, observing and absorbing, unsure if I had anything worth offering. But as I watched how he responded to others' feedback, I found myself pulled in, wanting to contribute, and questions started to come to me as others offered ideas. I hesitantly voiced one, and breathed a sigh of relief when it was met with his same enthusiastic reaction, reinforcing that what I had to say was worthwhile; I was encouraged to continue my contribution. Over a series of several meetings, the massive whiteboard became less blank space as more colored diagrams and words outlined our ideas for building this feature.

It wasn't the diagrams or the team's ideas that captivated me, but rather, our lead developer's ability to make everyone, including me, feel safe and compelled to contribute, regardless of our experience or perceived value. I loved how he treated every idea as if it was exceptional, or at least valid and well worth discussing; no idea was a bad idea. I looked forward to these meetings and came prepared with ideas and questions, wanting to provide value, and each time I left feeling proud to have contributed. Our lead developer had leaned into his **collaboration** superpower to encourage everyone to contribute, making everyone feel valued and appreciated, never silenced or judged.

After making sure I was more comfortable in my first IT auditor role, our manager recognized my interest in more than IT audit and offered me an opportunity to contribute in a different area. One morning, while in our weekly one-on-one meeting, she asked, "How would you feel about helping me audit entity-level controls?" This was an area she had owned up until then, and an area I knew little about, other than that fraud came up often. Auditing for fraud didn't sound very appealing to me, so I asked her if I could think about it and get back to her. She said of course, then directed me to our entity-level controls audit plan.

I went back to my desk and immediately started reviewing what entity-level controls were, and learned they are policies, rules, procedures and standards of behavior that apply to all members of an organization, from the board of directors to individual contributors. Some examples would be a company's mission statement, core values, code of conduct, employee handbook, internal complaint procedure, and employee review process. As I read through the information, I became more and more interested, understanding the contribution these controls make to a positive work culture. I stood up and almost ran back to her office to tell her I was in!

Later, when we hired a few additional auditors, our manager included me in the interview process, wanting my input on the candidates. After they were hired, she asked if I wanted to mentor them. Of course I said yes! I appreciated her leaning into her **empowerment** and **trust** superpowers, recognizing my interest in areas outside of IT audit, and offering me these additional opportunities to contribute.

———————————

Several months later, in my second IT auditor role, I was sitting in our weekly department meeting when I almost shouted in excitement, "I used that software in my last position!" Our manager had just announced the name of the audit software she was planning to implement, and it was the same software we had implemented right before I left my last company. I knew exactly how to use it! I held in my excitement until I met with her for our one-on-one meeting later that afternoon.

When we met, I could hardly wait to share that we had used the same software at my previous company and it had worked really well, and I was excited to use it again. Knowing I had software implementation experience from my consulting role, and recognizing my interest in project management, she asked me if I would be interested in leading our side of the implementation. "Your primary role will be communicating closely with the vendor and our team to make sure the implementation stays on track, and you'll need to balance this with your audit work." I forced myself to stay in my chair when what I really wanted to do was jump up and shout, "Yes!" I had wanted more responsibility, and this was perfect! Instead, I smiled widely and said, "Yes, I would love that," and thanked her for the opportunity. She had leaned into her **empowerment** and **trust** superpowers, recognizing my expertise in software implementations and my desire to do more, and provided a special way for me to contribute further, which eventually led to me moving into my first project management role at this same company.

Our project management team at the hospitality company had been busy managing projects using the processes, tools, and templates we had established and honed over a few years when our CEO called an emergency company meeting. As we gathered in the huge conference/break room, my nerves were on edge. I stood on my tiptoes, trying to see over the sea of heads in front of me as our CEO stood at the front of the room and shared slides announcing a pending acquisition. As he tried to reassure us that this was a good thing, my mind drifted. Past promises about similar acquisitions flashed before me and I decided it was time to start seeking my next role, confident the company's culture would be adversely impacted as I had seen with other companies going through acquisitions.

I started talking with a consulting company known for its positive work culture, which I believed in after having several conversations with their CEO and head of HR over several months. I left not long after the deal closed to take on a project manager role with this company, and a few months after I started, I was invited to join their Wellness Committee. I excitedly accepted, knowing it would feed my interest in both company and personal wellness. I really enjoyed planning and implementing wellness activities such as step challenges, mindfulness breaks, and healthy snacks. In fact, I enjoyed it more than my project manager role.

One afternoon I asked to talk with our CEO, and we ended up taking a walk outside. As we walked, the bitterly cold air took my breath away as well as my confidence. I frantically searched for the right words to let him know my passion was steering me toward helping people enjoy their jobs rather than software and technology projects, and I wondered if there were other opportunities within the company for me. He was very kind and listened attentively as I tried to communicate this, but he didn't have any immediate answers for me. A few weeks later, the individual leading the Wellness Committee left the company, and our CEO offered me the opportunity to take over leading the committee. I eagerly accepted this additional responsibility. He had heard me on our walk and leaned into his **empowerment** and **trust** superpowers to acknowledge my interests, providing an opportunity for me to contribute in an additional capacity. It wasn't perfect, but it did help.

Opportunities to Grow

On one of my first mornings at the accounting firm, our manager popped her head into the office I shared with my coworkers, looked directly at me, and asked, "Are you ready to go out on your first client visit?" My heart sped up, suddenly beating so fast I thought it was going to explode inside my chest. I did not feel ready to go out on my own! I looked at her, desperately trying to find words that wouldn't come. Then she smiled and said, "I'm going out to see one of my clients and wondered if you wanted to tag along." I let out a big sigh as my heart eased back into its normal pace, then I smiled and said, "Yes! I would love to!" hoping she hadn't noticed my panic but sure she had.

Shadowing her and our more senior consultant was an excellent way for our manager to ease me into client visits. By watching them, I learned not only our process for how to implement the accounting software but also how to interact with clients. This very quickly transitioned into me going out on my own, at first for small tasks, like a client requesting someone to come onsite to look into an issue instead of trying to resolve it over the phone. This was before the days of screen sharing tools, and if it was difficult for a client to describe exactly what was happening over the phone, they could request an onsite visit.

As I gained confidence through these smaller adventures, our manager assigned me to larger ones, helping a client through a specific part of an implementation, such as setting up general ledger accounts or entering in vendor or customer records. Finally, she trusted me to handle our biggest challenges, full implementations, including payables and payroll check runs, year-end closings, and upgrades to newer versions of the accounting software. Our manager leaned into her **empowerment** and **trust** superpowers, sending me on small assignments first, which helped me grow, gaining expertise and confidence in preparation for facing larger endeavors. Another way she helped me grow, which I have already mentioned, was by encouraging me to pursue my MBA, then fully supporting me in my pursuit.

Shortly after I moved into my first project management role at the insurance company, my new manager approached my desk. "I have a surprise for you!" he said with a wide grin. I wasn't sure what to think of him yet. I had only recently learned he was my manager after having interviewed with a different manager, reporting to him for only a few weeks before a reorganization. "What is it?" I asked hesitantly, trying to return his grin, unsure if it was a good surprise or something else. He proceeded to tell me, and it was a good surprise! The company was offering an onsite project management bootcamp to employees in a project management role or employees interested in project management, and he was recommending me! This bootcamp was an intensive week-long training and preparation course covering all phases of project management in the Project Management Body of Knowledge (PMBOK), a set of standard terminology and guidelines for project management. The goal of the bootcamp was to prepare attendees to take and pass the Project Management Professional (PMP) certification exam. "Thank you!" I said, grinning for real this time, thinking to myself, *This reorganization might turn out to be a good thing!*

For a week I joined several other lucky participants in a conference room, pouring over the many pages of the thick PMBOK with our instructor, who also walked us through how to complete the intense certification application, which included documenting time (hours) spent in project management roles. Then, Friday morning, we gathered to take our practice exam, a sample of the types of questions we could expect on the real exam. Before concluding the bootcamp, our instructor graded each exam and provided each of us with our results, pointing out areas we knew well and areas we should focus on before attempting the real exam.

For weeks after the bootcamp I worked on the application. I had reached out to both of my former audit managers to ask if they would support me in counting my audit hours as project management time. They both said yes. Even though I was no longer on their teams, they supported me and wanted to help me grow. After I completed the application I submitted it for approval, then I started studying. When I received notification that my application had been approved, I nervously scheduled my exam appointment.

The night before my exam I stayed up way too late reviewing my materials, hoping desperately I would pass. The next morning, I should have been exhausted, but I was wide awake as I sat in the small private room at the testing site reading and answering question after question. When I answered the last question I was about to hit the Submit button when a wave of appreciation for my new manager washed over me. He had leaned into his ***empowerment*** superpower and recommended me, a brand new member of his team, one that he hadn't even hired, for the bootcamp, wanting to provide me the opportunity to grow. *I really hope I pass*, I thought, as I took a deep breath and hit the Submit button. I waited, and waited, and finally the screen refreshed, displaying a Congratulations! message. I gathered up my things and walked out of the room to the exam proctor, a wide grin on my face. After I got home I emailed my new manager that I had passed, and then I took a long nap!

Having experienced the benefits of these and many other growth opportunities, I wanted to provide growth opportunities to my team members. Each of them came to my team with individual strengths as well as areas in which they needed time and space to grow. Stalwart Sage, Teamwork Titan, and I spent several weeks sequestered in conference rooms learning from each other before they took ownership of their agreed-upon products. Positivity Paladin learned our products as he worked on designs with each product manager and other team members. When Organized Oracle, Boomerang Brainiac, and Counselor QuickStudy joined our team, I leveraged the expertise of my existing team members to help them learn our products, processes, tools, and templates.

We had access to a robust online learning platform, but when it fell short of my team members' needs, I pushed for learning opportunities that were more meaningful to them. Each year I asked my team what learning opportunities or certifications they were interested in pursuing, then I advocated for them with Ironmind to get budget approval. I leaned into my **collaboration**, **empowerment**, and **trust** superpowers, wanting my team members to have opportunities to grow and to feel supported, both as they joined our team and as they became more seasoned team members.

Opportunities to Be Seen

In my first IT auditor role, our audit team separately documented findings as we performed our portion of the audit, each of us noting the deficiencies we found along with suggestions for how to address them.

At the end of the audit these findings were pulled into a consolidated audit report to be shared with the operating company's leadership team. Before sharing the report, our manager reviewed it carefully, to make sure the documented findings were written clearly and concisely. I will never forget how deflated I felt when I reviewed her comments after my first solo IT audit; the document was covered in red edits and comments like "I don't understand," "This is too technical," and "This is too long. Can you make it more concise?" Reflecting on this, it felt a lot like when I reviewed Jessica's edits after I submitted my first chapter draft for *Deserts to Mountaintops: Our Collective Journey to (re)Claiming Our Voice*, with red edits and "Show me! Don't tell me!" comments all over the document. With much patience from both of us, I learned to write a technical finding in a way that was easily understood by a nontechnical audience, and soon our manager's edits were less frequent, replaced with compliments on my ability to write a clear and concise finding.

When our manager finally deemed the audit report ready, our audit team met with the operating company's leadership team to deliver the report, with each of us taking a turn sharing what we had discovered in our portion of the audit. Our manager could certainly have done this meeting on her own, having become very familiar with our findings from her detailed review of the report, but she didn't. She gave us the opportunity to be seen as the experts in our audit areas. I didn't love this part of being an auditor, pointing out what people weren't doing well, and I was nervous every time it was my turn, worried about how the leaders would react, but it helped immensely having the support of our manager behind me, having reviewed and approved each of my findings. After the meetings, she often complimented me on my ability to deliver findings in a positive, nonthreatening way. I appreciated her leaning into her **collaboration**, **empowerment**, and **trust** superpowers to give me the opportunity to be seen, and to demonstrate my strong communication skills in this way.

From my early interactions with Frostgrip surrounding my first CliftonStrengths assessment, I was pretty sure accepting his offer had been a mistake. This feeling was firmly validated when I attended my first feature review meeting. In this recurring meeting, each member of Frostgrip's team would take a turn presenting their documentation on how a feature should look and act to the development team. This was meant to be an opportunity for the developers to learn about the feature and ask questions. However, what I witnessed was far from this expectation.

As I sat in the conference room surrounded by my coworkers, I couldn't help but notice the heavy demeanor of the first presenter. His dread was evident in his averted eyes, solemn face, tapping feet, and wringing hands. He could easily have shouted, "Get me out of here!" and it wouldn't have surprised me. Shortly after he started his presentation, I understood why.

I watched, astounded, my own sense of dread encasing me, as Frostgrip scoured the document displayed on the screen in front of us, looking for mistakes and weaknesses. His tone was sharp and cynical as he fired questions and statements at the presenter, "Where are they supposed to enter in the amount?" and "There is no way that will work!" His goal seemed to be to fluster and embarrass the presenter instead of trying to improve the document and feature, which should have been his goal. This did it for me. I had seen his true self—someone who took immense pleasure in making people uncomfortable, seizing every opportunity to attack, humiliate, and embarrass the presenter, to show he was in charge. This was not an opportunity to be seen. This was an opportunity to be ridiculed, and I wanted no part of it. I left the meeting and immediately started looking for my exit strategy.

Note: Although Frostgrip and Ironmind may sound like the same person, they are not. However, they do share similar personality traits. Perhaps they originated from the same celestial body.

Understanding how good it feels to be seen, I wanted to give my team members ample opportunities of their own. One way I did this was through the Good News/Best Professional/Best Personal and Status Updates agenda items in our team meetings, where they could share highlights of their own and their development teams' accomplishments with other members of our team. Another way was through my own and their quarterly and annual reviews, where I made a point to highlight my team's accomplishments, knowing they would be seen by HR and potentially by Ironmind.

A built-in opportunity for my team members to be seen was our biweekly sprint review meetings. In these meetings each product team would present the work they had completed over the past two weeks to company leaders and sales, services, and support team members. My team members presented in each of these meetings, describing the completed work items, introducing developers to demonstrate the completed work, and providing a sneak peek into tentative plans for the next sprint. Positivity Paladin showed designs he had completed and several times covered for out-of-office members of our team. I looked forward to these meetings, excited to see my team members showcase their skills and their development teams' work. They were always prepared, articulate, and engaging, and they publicly acknowledged the work their development teams had completed, helping their development team members be seen.

When my team attended a conference or an event, we would often put together a presentation to share at the next sprint review meeting. We started using a presentation tool Teamwork Titan had recommended, and one day we were working madly to get our highlights into this new tool in a flow that made sense before that afternoon's sprint review meeting. If someone had walked by our desks earlier in the day they would have seen our flurry of activity and panic, but no one would have suspected this had occurred later that afternoon when we presented at the meeting. By then we had worked together to create a beautiful presentation showcasing our experience. I really enjoyed listening to my team members share what they had learned during each conference or event they attended and was happy they had this special opportunity to be seen.

I had joined our People Committee early on and served as a member for a few years, enjoying planning and executing company events and wellness activities like I had as a member of the Wellness Committee at the consulting company. Due to a heavy workload I reluctantly gave up my spot, and when Teamwork Titan, also a member of the People Committee, resigned, I mentioned to Positivity Paladin that they might be looking for new members. I was expecting him to be excited about this, and he did not disappoint me. His face lit up with a bright smile as I told him with his positive energy and enthusiasm I thought he would be a great addition to the committee. He reached out almost immediately to the People Committee lead, who enthusiastically invited him to join the committee. I was excited he had the opportunity to be seen in this additional capacity.

In each of these examples, I leaned into my **collaboration**, **empowerment**, and **trust** superpowers to provide opportunities for my team members to be seen. I wanted others to see them as I did and to know how proud I was of them and what they could do. I loved seeing them shine. Although it was hard to see them leave my team, I was genuinely happy for Stalwart Sage and Teamwork Titan when they found new opportunities, knowing they had been seen by others who would hopefully appreciate them as much as I did.

OPTIMIZE SUPERPOWERS

Superpower	Activation
Collaboration	I lean into my **collaboration** superpower by creating an inclusive environment and ensuring equal air time for all team members. I listen attentively to understand and appreciate the input of others. I also acknowledge contributions and celebrate collaborative achievements.
Empowerment	I embrace my **empowerment** superpower by strategically delegating and granting autonomy over tasks. I enjoy recognizing and celebrating accomplishments while also providing the necessary resources and support for success. I promote continuous learning and encourage open communication.
Trust	Entrusting team members with challenging assignments and providing autonomy in decision-making is how I lean into my **trust** superpower. I like to maintain open and transparent communication, actively seeking input and feedback to show that I value other people's insights and perspectives.

OPTIMIZE WRAP-UP

In the wise words of business leadership author and inspirational speaker Simon Sinek: "A star wants to see himself rise to the top. A leader wants to see those around him rise to the top." Despite this quote's masculine tone, its essence is gender-neutral and aligns with the goal of this chapter. By leaning into your superpowers of **collaboration**, **empowerment**, and **trust** to let your team shine, you will create an environment where everyone feels empowered.

OPTIMIZE REFLECTION

1. Which superpowers really stood out to you in this chapter?
2. Which of these superpowers are most natural for you?
3. Which of these superpowers are most challenging for you?
4. Which story or stories in this chapter did you most relate to?
5. Which story or stories did you least relate to?
6. How do you encourage collaboration on your team?
7. What opportunities have you provided for your team members to be seen?
8. What are some ways you can Optimize: Let Your Team Shine?

CHAPTER 6

Nurture: Be Your Team's Biggest Fan

Nurture, as defined by Dictionary.com, means:

- "to feed and protect"
- "to support and encourage, as during the period of training or development; foster"

Appreciation

Although several of my managers were good at expressing appreciation, one really excelled in this area: my manager at the accounting firm. No matter what type of day I was having, whenever I found one of her handwritten notes intentionally placed on my desk, my mood was instantly elevated. Looking over to see a note from her on top of the stack of call printouts on my desk was always a highlight of my week. I never knew when it would appear, as the day and time varied, but I knew that although brief, it would be packed with appreciation. One particularly harried day, I was focusing on a call with a very nervous client when I saw movement in my peripheral vision. It was her, placing my stack on the corner of my desk. She saw that I was on a call, so she simply smiled, waved, and continued on her way. As I watched her leave, I thought, *Wow, how did she know?* Had she sensed from her office, several doors down the hall, that I needed to see her note today? Perhaps she was telepathic, like Mantis, sensing the needs of her Guardians of the Galaxy team members.

In all likelihood, she had sensed that we were all in need of an encouraging note that day. It was early January, and everyone was super busy, taking calls from panicked clients trying to get their year-end processes run successfully before the deadline. When I finished my call, I reached over and picked up my stack to read her note: "Ruth, You are doing a great job handling all of the year-end issues. I really appreciate the effort & patience you have given to our clients." A feeling of calm energy spread over me, as I smiled, put the stack down, and picked up the phone to take my next call. She had leaned into her **encouragement**, **enthusiasm**, and **gratitude** superpowers; she lifted my spirits and brightened my day.

On a warm sunny Saturday several years later, I was at our lake home, relaxing in our hammock under the canopy of shade trees, while taking a break from writing the first draft of my anthology chapter. I looked at my phone and noticed I had missed several messages from my coauthors. They were thanking Jessica for something, and I was intrigued but very confused, until one kindly shared a photo of her hand holding a silver circle mountain pendant necklace. When we got back to Fargo the next day, I dropped my bags in our living room and rushed to the front porch to see if there was anything from Jessica waiting for me. There was! I hurriedly but carefully opened the small envelope addressed to me, excited to see if what was inside matched what I had seen in the photo my coauthor had shared. Inside was a beautiful card with a handwritten note from Jessica, welcoming me to the anthology and thanking me for trusting her with my story. And inside the card was my own silver circle mountain pendant necklace, which I put on right away.

This was the first of many encouraging messages I received from Jessica throughout the anthology project. She often leaned into her superpowers of *encouragement*, *enthusiasm*, and *gratitude*, sending emails or WhatsApp messages to her coauthor team, thanking us for joining her, encouraging us as we wrote and edited our chapters, and celebrating us as we met deadlines. In return, we shared and celebrated our successes with each other, such as when we finished a draft, booked a chapter reading opportunity or convinced a bookstore, coffee shop, cider house, or yoga studio to stock and sell our book.

One brisk Friday afternoon as I was leaving our office building, an idea popped into my head. Instead of driving home as I had planned, I found myself steering my car toward Walmart, on a sudden mission to find something special to welcome my team members to their workspaces the following Monday. I wasn't exactly sure what that something special might be. I was hoping it would appear, as if by magic, and I would just know. I found what I was looking for, or at least the makings of what I was looking for, in a craft aisle. On the bottom shelf, there were several blank hanging wood signs that seemed to be beckoning to me. Above them were a variety of paints and stencils. Then an idea hit me: I could make us nameplates to hang outside our cubicles!

I had never stenciled before, so I spent some time pacing back and forth in the aisle, picking up the signs and putting them back, looking through the variety of paints and stencils, trying to decide if I could make these into that something special I was looking for. *What if they didn't turn out like I envisioned? What if my team members didn't like them?* I finally decided to go for it and purchased four signs, four different paint colors, stencils and sponges. The next morning I stood at our dining room table carefully making a nameplate for each of us, hoping they would turn out and breathing a huge sigh of relief as I removed the stencil from each one and saw the name revealed.

I arrived early at work the following Monday morning, excited to hang the nameplates outside each of our cubicles. As I hung each one, I imagined the team member arriving, seeing their new nameplate, and smiling, feeling a warm welcome and a reminder that they are a valued member of our team. I didn't watch to see their reactions as they arrived, but they did seem to like their nameplates, each thanking me in their own way. These nameplates hung outside our cubicles until we packed up and relocated to our homes due to COVID-19.

I loved leaning into my **encouragement**, **enthusiasm**, and **gratitude** superpowers like this, finding special ways to show my team members I appreciated them. I especially enjoyed browsing on Amazon or in local shops, seeking the perfect gift to celebrate a birthday, work anniversary, or special holiday. Often, I leaned into my Individualization strength, searching for a unique gift related to an individual's area of interest or a gift card to a place I knew they liked. Other times, I searched for a gift that was the same for everyone but had special meaning for our team, such as tumblers, coasters, or ornaments customized with pictures of our team we had taken while on a team outing or while celebrating Halloween.

I enjoyed showing appreciation for my team members through gifts, but I also enjoyed showing appreciation through words. I would often accompany a gift with a handwritten note, having learned how meaningful these were from my managers who did this for me. In these notes I tried to give an example of something specific I appreciated about them, such as their energy, determination, knowledge, passion, or sense of humor. According to the 5 Love Languages website, my love language is Words of Affirmation, so this makes perfect sense to me.

To include others in our celebrations, early in the morning on a team member's birthday or work anniversary, I would send an email to the people with whom they most interacted, encouraging them to wish my team member a happy birthday or happy anniversary, either in person, on a virtual meeting, or in a chat or email. I would often receive a heartfelt message at the end of the day from the celebrated team member, thanking me for making their day extra special.

One day I was in a virtual meeting with my team when our doorbell rang. This happened often, especially during and shortly after COVID-19, when we were doing most of our shopping online instead of in person. I was sure it was an Amazon package being delivered, with the delivery person just letting me know it was there, so I ignored it, planning to check after the meeting, but the ringing wouldn't stop. Finally, I asked my team to hold on and I ran downstairs to answer the door. A delivery person was standing on our porch, holding a bouquet of flowers. Surprised, I asked the delivery person if they had the right address. She smiled and nodded her head yes, pointing to the small envelope, with my name on it. Thanking her, I took the beautiful bouquet from her, and brought it upstairs with me. Before I rejoined the meeting, I peeked at what was inside the envelope, and a huge smile spread across my face. It was from my team! There were two notes inside, "Dear Ruth,

Happy Boss's day to someone who is never too busy to lend a hand, offer support, or answer a question." and "Dear Ruth, Thanks for the example you set and the support you give. You bring out the best in us all! Happy Boss's Day!" Beaming, I rejoined the call, basking in the warmth of my team leaning into their superpowers of **enthusiasm** and **gratitude**. I held up the bouquet and told them that they had made my day! I still have those cards, along with several handwritten birthday cards from them—thoughtful, meaningful expressions of appreciation that will always hold a special place in my heart.

Recognition

One cold and blustery evening in December, Dale and I were on a slow and careful drive to GPS's annual holiday party. I had been with the company for only a few months, and people had been telling me for weeks how fun the Holiday Wine & Cheese party was. I couldn't wait to spend some time with the people I had been spending most of my days with outside of work, and Dale was looking forward to meeting them, but the North Dakota winter storm outside was doing its very best to prevent us from attending. While Dale tried to focus on the slick icy streets becoming increasingly covered in snow, I was filling him in on who he might meet at the party. We finally arrived at the party venue and carefully made our way to the entrance, giggling as we tried hard not to fall on the slick ice and snow covered parking lot. Once we got inside, it was easy to tell where to go next from the loud music emanating from the huge conference room at the end of the hallway. As we walked in I looked around me, amazed. This was unlike any work party I had ever attended. The room was alive, buzzing with people, lights, and music. This was a party!

I scanned the room, looking for someone, anyone I recognized, but with the mass of people surrounding me I couldn't find anyone. Starting to feel dizzy from spinning around trying to find my people, I finally decided to give up my search and suggested we check out the food. I was expecting an assortment of cheeses and crackers, based on the name of the party, but what we found was a bounty of delicious food and snacks, including a huge bowl of popcorn mixed with plain M&Ms, something I had never tried before but have had many times since. Just as we spotted two empty chairs, the master of ceremonies (MC) stepped up to the microphone in the center of the stage at the far end of the room and announced, "Please find a seat! The show is about to start!" We rushed over to quickly sit down in the empty chairs before someone else did, as if we were playing a game of musical chairs and the music had just stopped.

The "show" was an elaborate awards ceremony, where the MC announced the names of several specially named awards, a brief description of what each award stood for, the list of nominees and a brief snippet of their nominations, and then the winner was announced, accompanied with a longer description of their nomination. Then the room exploded in applause and the lucky recipient stood and made their way to the stage to accept the specially designed trophy from the MC. I was charged by the excitement surrounding me, cheering as people I knew, people I knew of, and people I didn't know at all, excitedly made their way up to the stage to accept their awards. I loved the experience, drinking in the kind and appreciative words expressed in each nomination. The nominators had leaned into their superpowers of *encouragement* and *gratitude*, committing time to craft thoughtfully written words of encouragement and appreciation about people they spent most of their days with. I made a mental note to submit at least one nomination the next time I had an opportunity.

After the awards ceremony, the MC announced and welcomed a band to the stage. Dale and I looked at each other and smiled. We both love to dance! As the night went on, we rotated between dancing and mingling with my coworkers. Then we slowly and carefully made our way back home on the snow-covered roads.

Several years later, a few months after I rejoined GPS and Dale and I moved back to Fargo, Dale and I attended a much smaller version of the Holiday Wine and Cheese party, one focused on our global development team. Again I was charged by the excitement surrounding me, cheering as people I knew, people I knew of, and people I didn't know excitedly made their way up to the stage to accept their awards. When the MC announced the Rookie of the Year award I leaned forward, excited to see the list of nominees, and I was surprised to see my name appear in the list on the screen above him. Before I could really comprehend it, I heard my name announced, "Ruth Hetland!" and the screen changed, flashing only my name on the display. I couldn't believe it! I was the Rookie of the Year! I couldn't have stopped the huge smile from spreading across my face if I had tried. I looked over at Dale and slowly stood, thankful I had bought a new dress for the evening. Everyone's eyes were now focused on me. I glanced over at my manager, who was at a nearby table, and as our eyes met, she smiled and mouthed "Congratulations!" As I walked toward the stage to accept my award, a feeling of warmth enveloped me like a winter blanket.

I carefully made my way up to the stage, maneuvering around the maze of large round tables filled with smiling people cheering me on. When I reached the stage, the MC handed me my award, a small glass globe atop a black marble base, titled "Rookie of the Year," with my name, and the year etched into it. Surprised joy burst out of me as I took the award from the MC, thanked him, and made my way back to my seat.

The award was beautiful, but what meant more to me were the nominations the MC handed me with the award. When I got back to my seat, I glanced through the pages, but I wanted to wait until I got home to thoroughly absorb them. Later at home that night, dressed in my favorite comfy lounge pajamas, I relaxed into a cozy cup of spiced hot chocolate as I settled into my sofa to read the nominations. There were several, both from my peers and my manager. Every single one held thoughtful sentiments noting how quickly I had caught on and contributed to the team and company. One nomination in particular stood out to me. It was from a developer I had been working closely with for several weeks, someone I really enjoyed working with, who I had nominated for an award as well. I smiled as I read his nomination. "I'm not sure where Ruth came from, but I am so glad she is here!" He went on to say how thought provoking my questions were and that I really cared about our products and customers. I crawled into bed that night, with that huge smile still stretched across my face. My manager and my peers had leaned into their *encouragement* and *gratitude* superpowers, taking time to write and submit meaningful and impactful nominations. I fell asleep feeling appreciated and valued.

Several years later, at the consulting company I worked at prior to joining NAGPS, I learned that Fridays were special recognition days. This company was founded and led by former GPS team members, who understood the importance of recognizing team members for their accomplishments. Every Friday morning we gathered together for an all company meeting, and the first agenda item was always Kudos, a special time for team members to recognize and celebrate other team members. Throughout the week we could submit Kudos about other team members, and whoever led the meeting, usually our president, would announce each Kudo, who it was for, and who submitted it, then turn it over to the submitter, to elaborate on the Kudo they had written.

One Friday morning I was especially excited for our Kudos session. I had recently read Patrick Lencioni's latest book, *The Ideal Team Player: How to Recognize and Cultivate the Three Essential Virtues: A Leadership Fable*. In this book, Lencioni references a concept from Jim Collins's book *Good to Great: Why Some Companies Make the Leap . . . And Others Don't*: getting "the right people on the bus," a euphemism for hiring and retaining employees who fit a company's culture. He then shares that "the right people" are the ones who have three virtues in common: humility, hunger, and people smarts. As I sped through the book, soaking up every detail like a sponge, I visualized several great people I worked with, but one kept coming to the forefront, a functional consultant on one of my projects. I absolutely loved working with her, and it was suddenly clear to me why: she exemplified humility, hunger, and people smarts. When I finished the book, I picked up my laptop and typed up a Kudo for her, listing examples of how she demonstrated these three virtues. That Friday morning I could hardly wait for our all-company meeting, excited to share this Kudo with her and the rest of the company. I loved seeing people embrace their ***encouragement***, ***enthusiasm***, and ***gratitude*** superpowers, recognizing team members who had made a positive impact on their week, and I loved having this unique opportunity to do the same.

Danger: Favoritism

Although I often leaned into my Individualization strength to celebrate my team members, I made it a priority to spread my appreciation and recognition evenly across the entire team. I never wanted anyone to feel that I had favorites. This was not a priority Ironmind and I shared. Ironmind had obvious favorites, which he did not try to hide.

Shadowwit, who you met earlier, was one of Ironmind's favorites. Ironmind made this evident by showering Shadowwit with frequent praise and reserving his toxic criticism for others.

One cool, fall evening in September, about nine months before my layoff, Dale and I were at a work gathering at our office building. It was one of the first Fargo team gatherings we had been to since the majority of our office had relocated to our homes due to COVID-19. Dale and I were coming outside to get in line for the food truck they had brought in when Ironmind arrived. As he walked toward us, he had a big smile on his face and he waved, which surprised me, but I smiled and waved back. As he got closer I realized he wasn't smiling or waving at us. Shadowwit and his wife were right behind Dale and me, and Ironmind walked right past Dale and me, as if we were both invisible, and immediately started talking with them. We got in line, and I foolishly expected him to acknowledge us at some point. He didn't. We ordered our food, went inside and ate, and I watched them sit across the room, talking amongst themselves as if they were the only ones in the room the entire night.

A few weeks before my layoff, I signed into our virtual leadership team meeting and was surprised to discover we had additional attendees. We had recently acquired another company, and several of our new team members were attending this meeting, which Ironmind mentioned after everyone arrived. Ironmind acknowledged the new team members, then asked each of us to introduce ourselves. However, before we could give our introductions, he felt the need to make his own introduction for each of us. When it was my turn, he cleared his throat before saying, "Ruth, how long have you been here? Has it been five years yet?" I took a deep breath and put my hand up to my cheek, checking to see if his verbal slap had indeed left a mark. I replied that I had been there six and a half years, but what I wanted to say was, "How do you not know that? You signed my five-year anniversary card a year and a half ago! Why did you even say anything if that's all you could think of to say about me?" I swallowed hard and proceeded with my introduction, trying not to show how much his lack of interest in me hurt. I shared a bit of my extensive background, then gave a brief introduction and shout out to each one of my team members, who were not in attendance. When I finished, Ironmind introduced Shadowwit, sharing how he and Shadowwit had known each other for years, having both worked at a different software company and noting how he had actively recruited Shadowwit to our company. I tuned out the rest of his praise as I slowly slunk into my chair, deflated and feeling invisible. I wondered if anyone else was tired of hearing this song.

Basking in the glow of Ironmind's praise, Shadowwit proceeded with his introduction. As I listened to him, I reflected on two interactions with him that I will never forget. Late one afternoon, a coworker and I were in a meeting with Shadowwit, and he disagreed with something we were discussing. Instead of talking calmly through the issue, as my colleague and I were attempting to do, he lost it. He stood up suddenly, threw his pen across the table—thankfully missing both of us—and stormed out of the room. We looked at each other, stunned and speechless, unable to move or believe what had just happened. It was as if we had just witnessed Dr. Bruce Banner turning into the Hulk, except he had turned red instead of green. When I regained my voice, I said, "I will go try to talk to him." I approached him at his desk, and asked, "Can we talk?" He replied gruffly, "No, I need to get out of here!" Then he stood up, stormed past me, and left the office. Well aware that Shadowwit was a favorite of Ironmind, and we had nowhere to safely turn, my colleague and I tried to forget about the incident and move on, but we were both careful around him from then on, never knowing when a similar fit of rage might materialize.

Several weeks later, I was at a team dinner and somehow got seated next to Shadowwit. After a long, uncomfortable side-by-side dinner, as the evening wound down, he looked over and said, "I'm sorry about losing my temper before." I knew exactly what he was referring to, but I was also confused, because it had been so long since the incident. I thanked him for apologizing, feeling as if I had no other choice. It felt ingenuine, like he had been told he should apologize and wanted to report back that he had.

Things were better, for a while. Then, a few weeks before I was laid off, I was in a virtual meeting with just Shadowwit. I was asking him questions, trying to understand something he was proposing, when his rage suddenly returned. To avoid a complete recurrence of our previous incident, I lowered my voice and talked calmly, as if I was Black Widow trying to calm down the Hulk. I was very tempted to say, "Hey, big guy. The sun's getting real low." Again, knowing he was one of Ironmind's favorites and I had nowhere to turn that seemed safe, I kept this to myself, resolving to be even more careful in future interactions with him.

Shadowwit wasn't Ironmind's only favorite; he was just the favorite I interacted with most. Ironmind had other favorites, a few other friends he had recruited and hired, and a few young, attractive women, who he told me once he enjoyed mentoring. I was not young, which he liked to point out, having somehow found out we were close in age. One memory I cannot erase no matter how hard I try: We were in a one-on-one meeting, and he was reflecting on a recent surgery he had undergone: hooded eyelid surgery. As he was filling me in on what the surgery involved, which I had no interest in learning, he casually mentioned that he could tell I would likely need the same surgery soon. I had no response.

NURTURE SUPERPOWERS

Superpower	Activation
Encouragement	I embrace my ***encouragement*** superpower by providing genuine and specific praise for efforts and achievements. I use positive reinforcement and celebrate successes and milestones, striving to tailor my approach to each person in a way that resonates with them personally.
Enthusiasm	By demonstrating genuine excitement and passion for my team members, I lean into ***enthusiasm***. I like to celebrate achievements regularly, recognizing both individual and team successes, with the goal to foster a sense of accomplishment and pride throughout my team.
Gratitude	I lean into my ***gratitude*** superpower by expressing thanks sincerely and specifically, acknowledging the efforts and contributions of others in a meaningful way. I use thank-you notes, verbal acknowledgments, and thoughtful gestures to express my appreciation.

NURTURE WRAP-UP

As Ralph Marston, renowned motivational speaker, author, and personal development expert, wisely said, "Make it a habit to tell people thank you. To express your appreciation, sincerely and without the expectation of anything in return. Truly appreciate those around you, and you'll soon find many others around you." This quote is a perfect representation of what this chapter is about. By leaning into your superpowers of ***encouragement***, ***enthusiasm***, and ***gratitude*** to be your team's biggest fan, you will create an environment where everyone feels valued.

NURTURE REFLECTION

1. Which superpowers really stood out to you in this chapter?
2. Which of these superpowers are most natural for you?
3. Which of these superpowers are most challenging for you?
4. Which story or stories in this chapter did you most relate to?
5. Which story or stories did you least relate to?
6. What has made you feel appreciated and/or recognized?
7. How would you have responded to Ironmind's favoritism or Shadowwit's rage?
8. What are some ways you can Nurture: Be Your Team's Biggest Fan?

NURTURE

Story and illustration by Nathan Long

CHAPTER 7

Gambol: Have Fun with Your Team

Gambol, as defined by Dictionary.com, means:

- "to skip about, as in dancing or playing; frolic"

Water Fun

"Did you bring your suit?" It was early evening when the owner poked his head into the doorway between the store where I was working and the shop where he was working to ask me this very important question. He had a wide grin on his face as he waited for my answer, and I felt a similar grin spreading across my own face. "Yes!" I almost shouted. I loved hearing those five words!

My second job, a few years after my ill-fated, short-lived first job at the drugstore cafe, was at a resort located between two of Minnesota's 10,000 lakes. I worked at this resort the summer after I graduated from high school through the summer after I graduated from college. I was hired to work in the small grocery store/gas station next to the owner's repair shop where he had a constant flow of small engine repair work. The owner was an elementary school teacher during the school year and ran the resort during the summer. A few weeks after I started, he came into the store in his standard uniform: T-shirt, cutoff jean shorts, and bare feet, and told me, "Bring your suit to work tomorrow." I looked up from the cash register to see if he was serious. "My suit? Do you mean my swimsuit?" I was perplexed. I couldn't picture myself ringing up customers' groceries in a swimsuit! "Why?" I immediately grew nervous, thinking he had some awful job in or around the water waiting for me. I had learned quickly that when it was slow in the store, he would find other tasks for me. These had so far included using a squeegee and buckets of soapy water to remove dead fishfly carcasses from the windows and pop machines outside the store entrance and adding a fresh coat of paint to weather-beaten storm window frames in early preparation for winter, all while watching and listening for the occasional customer.

At least the fish flies were dead by the time I had to interact with them. The worst thing he ever asked me to do was package leeches. The first time he showed me how to do this, I had to swallow hard to keep from gagging as I watched him reach into the white, five-gallon pail filled with murky water and a huge, writhing black blob of slime. He then proceeded to pull out a handful of squirming leeches, bigger than I had ever seen, and counted out loud as he dropped them, barehanded, one by one, into the awaiting styrofoam cup already filled with water. He repeated this until he had thirteen leeches in the cup, one more than a dozen. After covering the cup with a plastic lid, he looked up at me and asked, "Do you think you can do this?" I asked, trying hard not to show how repulsed I was, "Can I use a scoop like I use for the minnows?" He rolled his eyes and laughed at me, then stood up and walked away. I stood there, assuming that was a no, trying to build up the nerve to reach into that bucket. Then, to my surprise, he returned and handed me a scoop.

I was worried when he told me to bring my swimsuit that he was going to make me harvest leeches, realizing I didn't know where those leech-filled buckets had actually come from. Instead, and to my total surprise, he explained, "It's supposed to be nice tomorrow night, and if it's slow, we're going to take the boat out and I'm going to teach you how to ski." I was excited and terrified at the same time. Besides being an elementary school teacher and the resort owner, he was also a champion water skier. I had seen him ski, on regular skis, a slalom ski, trick skis, and barefoot; he was the master, and I had never even tried on a pair of skis!

I should have known I had nothing to be afraid of. He was a kind and patient teacher, showing me how to put the skis on, then guiding me with easy-to-follow instructions. "Bend your knees to keep the tips out of the water, hold onto the rope, and slowly stand up!"

After several tries, I was successful in standing up, finally feeling the boat pull me out of the water. I skied for a few yards, then wiped out, letting go of the rope as soon as I felt unsteady, just as he had taught me. After a few more tries, I was able to get back up and skied for a short distance before letting go of the rope; my hand, arm, and leg muscles were too tired to continue. After making sure I was done with my turn, he took his. He was mesmerizing to watch, jumping expertly across the wake and forming a huge water spray as he turned to cross again. He dropped one ski, then the other to ski barefoot, then turned around to ski backward. But more than the incredible talent and skill he displayed, what I remember most about that night was the joy all over his face.

By the end of that summer, we had done this several times; cutting out early to go ski on the lake when things were slow. I learned to ski not only on two skis, but also how to drop one to slalom ski. I even learned how to get up on a slalom ski. To this day, I have never gone back to skiing on two skis.

One perfectly warm and sunny Minnesotan summer afternoon, my sister, who had joined me to work at the resort, and I had the day off. We asked the owner if we could rent the windsurfs the resort kept available for customers. He shook his head no and said, "You can't rent them." Crestfallen, we did our best to hide our disappointment, but were heartened when he smirked and followed up with, "You can just use them. I won't charge you."

Then, he demonstrated how to use them, balancing on the board as he pulled up the sail, maneuvering it to catch the wind, allowing the air to propel the board across the water. We were so excited when we finally mastered this ourselves, after several tries and wipeouts. We took off, easily propelling across the water toward the other side. We were having a blast until we realized, too late, more than halfway across the lake, that we had no idea how to get back. We tried to use the sails to catch the wind in the opposite direction, but we were unsuccessful, and we ended up moving even further toward the other shore. We tried to paddle back, but our progress was very slow with the sails dragging in the water behind us. Then we saw the owner approaching in his boat. He had been watching our struggle from the shore and had come to our rescue. Exhausted from the struggle, we climbed into his boat and asked the questions we should have asked before, about getting back to shore. Not once did he make us feel embarrassed, but he did tease us often about our little windsurf misadventure.

When I am asked about my favorite job, I often mention this one, for three reasons: First, it was fun to welcome happy vacationers into the store and help them find what they were looking for. Second, the variety; I enjoyed the odd jobs, even packaging the leeches, once I had my scoop, and third, I appreciated the owner. He often leaned into his superpowers of **creativity**, **humor**, and **playfulness**, not only sharing his time and resources to provide us with after hours fun, but also sharing his sense of humor during work hours, making our jobs more enjoyable. I still love to water ski, but I have never windsurfed again! I love to paddleboard though, especially since I know exactly how to get back to shore.

"Yay! Tomorrow is Lake Day!" I heard several variations of this phrase uttered at GPS one summer afternoon after Dale and I had moved back to Fargo. My energy matched my coworkers' as we prepared to leave for the day. Knowing the next day was technically a workday, but would be spent at the lake in the warm summer sun was indeed something to look forward to! After surviving another frigid, snow-covered North Dakota winter followed by another drizzly, mud-covered spring, I was craving the warmth of the sun like I imagine Captain America did after he was found and defrosted seventy years after crashing into the Arctic.

The head of our department was hosting a lake day at his summer house; we were all excited about an afternoon of sun, water sports, yard games, food, snacks, and beverages. That night as I selected sunscreen, sunglasses, a hat, and a towel to pack into a bag, my hands rested on my swimsuit, wondering if I should pack it. I had heard there was a speedboat, and I did love water skiing, but as I pictured myself standing in front of my coworkers in a swimsuit, my decision was made. I left my swimsuit in the drawer.

The next morning I woke up early, excited to spend time away from the office, relaxing in the sun with my coworkers. As I watched the activity on the lake later that afternoon, I knew I had made the right decision. No one was water skiing. They were tubing, and I do not enjoy tubing. I could picture myself on the tube, hanging onto the handles for dear life, bouncing around like a rag doll, desperately trying not to lose my grip and launch off the tube, ricocheting across the water surface like a skipped rock. That was not my idea of a good time. I was happy staying on the sunny shore, feasting on yummy food, and playing bocce ball.

Our department head had leaned into his superpowers of *creativity*, *humor*, and *playfulness*, providing a fun way for our entire team to escape the office for a day and enjoy the warm summer weather—such a rare treat in our area. Every year, he graciously hosted these lake days, bringing us closer together with recreation and relaxation, allowing us to interact in a casual setting with colleagues we worked closely with and connect with those we didn't interact with as often.

"Huh, huh, huh, huh, huh, huh, huh, huh." Her low, slow chuckle came from the front of the boat, echoing back to me. My hands, struggling to keep my body on the seat, occasionally lost the fight and I would be launched crazily into the air with each big wave, as if gravity had momentarily vanished.

Our audit manager also had a summer lake home, and when she invited her entire team and their significant others out for a day at the lake, we jumped at the chance. The weather wasn't sunny and warm, but rather rainy and cool, which could have put a damper on our day, but she didn't let it. She made the most of the day by providing delicious food and organizing indoor games while the rain poured down outside.

When there was a break in the rain, we all packed into the boat for a short ride before it started again. I heard her familiar chuckle as the rain started up again, and not just a sprinkle, but a straight up downpour! Our manager's husband did his best to get us back to land as fast as he could, dodging waves as they tried to slow his progress. She sat beside him, chuckling. We were all soaked when we returned, and as we climbed out of the boat, I noticed everyone was smiling, happy to be back on land, but also having enjoyed the wild ride.

Our manager had leaned into her superpowers of **creativity**, **humor**, and **playfulness**, giving us a fun day out of the office, away from thinking about operating company audits. She also expertly demonstrated how even when things are challenging, you can remain positive and enjoy the experience, which she did by not letting the weather alter her plans for a fun and bonding team experience.

I can host my own lake day! I thought after we bought our lake home. By the next summer, with personal touches added to make it feel like ours, I was ready. I messaged the Synergy Squad, "Who's up for a lake day?" The replies were instant: "Yes!"

We were all working remotely at the time, but everyone lived within driving distance and was eager to make the trip. We found a Friday in mid-September, knowing it might be cool, but we were determined to make it work.

Our lake home is just ten minutes from a small tourist town, so we met there for lunch at a local spot famous for its burgers. As we munched on burgers, sandwiches, fries, and salads, we caught up on our weeks and weekend plans. After lunch, we strolled the main street, stopping to browse a few shops. Organized Oracle, who was moving to the East Coast soon, was on a quest for a sweatshirt as a keepsake. She found one, slipped it on immediately—it was sunny but cool—and we headed to the lake.

When we arrived, I couldn't wait to show them the new pullup bar in our garage gym. "I'll give you each a T-shirt if you attempt a pullup!" I teased, chuckling. Positivity Paladin and Stalwart Sage gamely gave it a try before we moved on to the house. I showed them around, excited to reveal our sunroom-turned-yoga room to Teamwork Titan, our newly certified yoga instructor. "I'll do a yoga pose for a T-shirt!" she laughed, striking her best warrior pose to our applause.

After a leisurely boat ride around the lake, Dale snapped a few group photos for us. Then we said our goodbyes, and I wished everyone a safe drive home. It was a fun, relaxing day, made even more special by Organized Oracle's upcoming move. I loved leaning into my *creativity*, *humor*, and *playfulness* superpowers to bring everyone together. After they left, I hopped online and ordered T-shirts for each of them, complete with our Golden Pond Gym logo.

Scary Fun

"Quiet! Here he comes!" We quickly ran to our desks and sat down, eagerly waiting for our coworker to walk into the office. Despite his fun sense of humor, he had refused to dress up for Halloween, so we decided to play a trick on him. When he walked in we all had our backs to him. As he approached each of our desks, we slowly turned, revealing our hideous faces. Someone had learned he didn't like clowns, so we had all dressed up, not just as clowns, but as scary clowns. I heard a wave of screams as he made his way through our office, encountering scary clown after scary clown. When I sensed him nearing my desk, I turned around, and he screamed again! It took everything I had to hold my laughter in, but I was committed to this prank.

When he reached his own desk, we followed him and gathered nearby, removing our masks after one final fright to make sure he was okay. Thankfully, he was. He slumped over his desk, tears streaming down his face, laughing. Everyone, including him, had leaned into their *courage*, *creativity*, *humor*, and *playfulness* superpowers to have fun together as a team.

"Huh, huh, huh, huh, huh, huh, huh, huh." Her low, slow chuckle echoed around me once again, like it had on our wild boat ride back to her lake place, but this time it disappeared into the screams and shrieks surrounding us as we plunged into darkness. My body, momentarily weightless, couldn't keep my stomach from fluttering in protest as it fought to keep up with our rapid descent. I will never forget those sounds or that feeling, and I will never stop smiling when I recall them. That low, slow chuckle came from my very brave manager as we fell from high up on the The Twilight Zone Tower of Terror ride at Disney World. We were attending an audit conference in Orlando, and we had decided to check out Disney-MGM Studios (now Disney's Hollywood Studios) on our one free, sticky-hot evening. Always a thrill seeker (I love amusement parks!) I somehow had managed to convince everyone, including our manager, to ride this terrifying attraction.

I love scary rides, especially those that produce that stomach-flipping-I'm-about-to-lose-my-lunch sensation! I don't think my manager really wanted to ride the Tower of Terror, but somehow I convinced her and the rest of my team to go on it not once, but three times. Each time we safely reached the main floor of the haunted hotel after unexpectedly dropping, rising, and dropping again from stories above, I smiled and shouted "Again!" like a toddler addicted to flying! Finally, after the third round (although I would have ridden again!) I agreed to move on. I could almost hear everyone's huge sigh of relief!

Several weeks later, our manager paid me back when we visited a power plant owned by one of our operating companies. We stood several stories above the main floor, facing a huge metal grate that opened to the vast space below. My manager had carefully tiptoed her way out into the middle, urging each of us to join her for a view of how far up we were. I could hardly make myself look at the floor below from the solid surface I was standing on, let alone venture out into the middle!

Ironically, while I love rides that drop, I hate heights. I know that seems contradictory, but it feels less terrifying when someone else controls my rise and fall. Climbing a high ladder or walking up see-through steps is nearly impossible for me, especially if I look down. My limbs freeze, and I start to hyperventilate, convinced I will lose my grip or trip and fall to a tragic end. Just thinking about stepping onto that huge metal grate gave me the same sensation. In fact, my fingers are starting to numb as I recall it right now! Chills run up and down my spine, locking up my fingers and toes.

But because she had leaned into her superpowers of *courage*, *humor*, *open-mindedness*, and *playfulness* for me—going on the Tower of Terror ride not once, but three times—I knew I had to do it. I stepped carefully onto the grate, hugging the edge. I glanced down, then quickly looked up at her, hoping I had passed her test. After seeing her encouraging and validating smile, I stepped off just as quickly, retreating as far from that metal grate as possible, as if it might reach out and pull me back. She joined me back on solid ground and said with a smile, "I can't believe that after three rides on the Tower of Terror, this freaks you out!" Her low, slow chuckle returned.

I smiled back, grateful to be safe—and grateful for her. She had playfully challenged me to face my fear and supported me the entire way, helping me lean into my own superpowers of **courage**, **humor**, **open-mindedness**, and **playfulness**, along with **humility**. I felt a sense of camaraderie built from facing our fears together and realized she would be there when I needed someone to lean on in moments of risk or fear.

Dress-Up Fun

"What should our Halloween theme be?" our audit manager asked us in our weekly department meeting. Halloween was quickly approaching, and each department at the insurance company was encouraged to pick a theme, decorate their department's space, and dress up. Several ideas were tossed about, and we all agreed that Clue was the best one. I rushed home that day to pull out our Clue game, having volunteered to bring it in so we could study the game board, weapons, and characters.

Over the next couple of weeks, our department was a flurry of activity as we determined which areas in our department would become which Clue rooms, trying to work as much as possible with what we already had. For example, our manager's cubicle would be The Library, with her big bookshelf filled with books. After designing our game board, we spent several lunch breaks gathering supplies to transform each area into the Clue room of our vision. We also made sure we had Clue weapons available, bringing in items from our homes, including a rope, a wrench, and a lead pipe. We each selected a Clue suspect, and gathered the necessary items on our own to become that character. I was to be Mrs. White, the prim and proper maid. I had fun assembling the perfect costume: a long-sleeved black dress, a ruffled white apron with straps, and a white-haired wig pulled into a bun.

The day before Halloween we worked diligently to transform our space into a replica of the game board, and on Halloween we each arrived dressed as our characters. I was excited to show off my costume, but I had some serious competition! I barely recognized some of my teammates; they had truly transformed into their roles. Throughout the day we welcomed other departments into our space, inviting them to first view the Clue game we had set out and then step into the live version we had created. Everyone seemed to really enjoy their visit, bringing huge smiles to our Clue character faces. It was such a fun day!

Our manager had leaned into her superpowers of **creativity**, **humor**, **humility**, and **playfulness**, joining us in every step of planning, decorating, and dressing up, leading to a uniquely fun Halloween celebration. That evening, as I took off my costume, I was still smiling, reflecting on the entire experience and appreciating how our manager had shown everyone that it is okay to have fun at work.

"I don't like to look silly," Ironmind said, his grimace clearly showing his discomfort, when I mentioned that my team and I were dressing up for Halloween, and, against my better judgment, I had invited him to join in. As I walked away from our abrupt conversation, I wondered if he was really saying, "You shouldn't look silly." But I decided I wasn't going to worry about his opinion. As a member of the People Committee, I wanted celebrating Halloween to become an important tradition in our office. I had seen, in other companies, how it fostered collaboration and communication, bringing teams closer and helping colleagues get to know each other. Plus, I really wanted to dress up with my team.

We had decided to be X-Men, and while we did invite others to join us, only a few did; most did not. We had met as a team to review the X-Men characters, each selecting which one we wanted to be. To study up on our characters, someone suggested we go together to see *X-Men: Dark Phoenix*, so one afternoon we left work early to catch the movie. Because it was a weekday matinee, the theater was empty except for us, making it feel like our own private viewing party. We laughed as we watched the characters come to life on the big screen, pointing out traits each of us should emulate to embrace our character. It was a fun afternoon, and as I walked to my car after saying goodbye to everyone, I was glad we had taken the opportunity to bond over such a fun research project. I smiled, excited to dress up and be silly with them.

A few days later, I got up early to morph myself into Quicksilver. I showed up clad in black jeans and a Pink Floyd T-shirt, accessorized with a black faux leather jacket with silver accents and silver tennis shoes. To complete the picture, I had even spray painted my hair silver. I walked into our office building with confidence, excited to see the rest of my team's transformations. They did not disappoint. Waiting for me were Angel/Archangel (Positivity Paladin), Rogue (Teamwork Titan), and Phoenix (Stalwart Sage). We had a really fun day leaning into our characters, and from that day on, dressing up as a team for Halloween became our thing.

One cool fall Saturday morning a few years later, I was sitting at our lake home, looking through pictures on my phone. The night before we had rewatched the movie *Inside Out*, and as I looked at one of the last pictures I had taken with my dad before he passed away earlier that year, I realized I was wearing the same sweater as Sadness. Seeing Sadness in the same sweater felt strangely fitting, as if we shared a unique bond, a quiet reminder of my dad.

Halloween was quickly approaching, and although I knew I should probably wait until Monday, I was just too excited. I opened up the Teams app on my phone and went into our team chat. I pasted in a picture of the *Inside Out* characters and a picture of me with my dad, wearing the Sadness sweater, and typed, "Inside Out for Halloween this year? I already have the Sadness sweater!" Then I closed the app, not expecting anyone to respond until Monday.

Within a few seconds, a message indicator appeared on my phone, and I peeked at it. Stalwart Sage had replied with one word, "Joy!" Then Teamwork Titan replied, "I can be Disgust! I can use some of my green clothing from my Rogue and Spring costumes!" We had dressed up as the four seasons (Spring, Summer, Fall, Winter) for a previous Halloween. Positivity Paladin joined in, committing to being Anger, which seemed incredibly ironic since I'm not sure I've ever seen him angry, which left Organized Oracle with Fear, which she willingly accepted. Within a few minutes of me sending my message, they had all fully engaged and selected their characters. I smiled, feeling a warmth I hadn't expected—their enthusiasm lightened any heaviness I had been feeling earlier.

A year later, when our team had morphed into the New Synergy Squad, I read a message in my Teams chat: "What should we be for Halloween this year?" My heart leapt. The message was from Positivity Paladin to our team, and it made me smile. I was hoping my new team members would share our enthusiasm for dressing up as a team as I added "Halloween" to our next team meeting agenda and replied to his message, asking everyone to bring their ideas to the meeting.

When we met a few days later, the team came with several ideas, and we decided as a group to be Scooby-Doo. When we finished selecting which character we each wanted to be, Counselor QuickStudy, our newest team member exclaimed, "I didn't realize what a fun team I was joining!" A huge smile spread across my face.

I loved brainstorming and collaborating with my team about Halloween themes and costumes. We became the team to beat in costume contests, but more important to me was the way we came together and had fun. Leaning into our *creativity*, *humor*, *humility*, *open-mindedness*, and *playfulness* superpowers did more than just create a fun tradition; it created an environment where everyone could be themselves, embracing silliness as well as seriousness, supported by trust and mutual respect.

Virtual Fun

"Did your breakfast arrive yet?" I anxiously asked each time a team member joined our virtual meeting. We had originally planned to meet in person for breakfast that morning to check out a new restaurant specializing in coffee and waffles, but due to COVID-19 restrictions, we had to pivot to a virtual gathering. I felt a mix of excitement and apprehension about this new way of connecting, because it was our first team gathering since relocating to our homes. I wanted everyone to feel comfortable connecting, despite our physical distance.

The day before, I had gathered breakfast orders from each team member and called the restaurant, explaining my goal to have each order delivered around the same time. The restaurant staff was incredibly accommodating, enlisting both their delivery drivers and employees to meet my needs.

Once everything was set in motion, the real test began during our online gathering. Despite a few delays, everyone received their breakfast orders while we connected online, allowing us to share the delicious aroma of freshly brewed coffee and the sight of warm, fluffy waffles. It felt almost as if we were gathered in person, sharing not just food but also laughter and conversation. I counted this as a success, reinforcing our team bond even as we embarked on this new virtual adventure. This experience made me realize that, even from a distance, we could still create meaningful connections.

As our team grew and we transitioned fully and permanently to being a remote team spread across several locations, I wanted to maintain this feeling of connection. Our regular meetings were now virtual, and we became experts at interacting online rather than in person. Just as we made the most of our virtual breakfast, we also found creative ways to celebrate special occasions and holidays, such as Halloween. We gathered to show off our costumes and finished with team photos to share with others, which became even more fun as Microsoft introduced new Teams background tools. For example, we used the Together Mode feature with a background of a creepy haunted house wall, decorated with frames draped in spider webs, to capture a Scooby-Doo team photo.

Through our virtual celebrations, we discovered the joy of virtual games, with Scattergories becoming one of our favorites. Our People Committee also embraced the virtual game world by planning holiday celebrations for everyone, which often included virtual trivia games with questions centered around the holiday we were celebrating. I enjoyed the opportunity to have fun with both the team members I worked closely with and those I rarely interacted with in other areas of our rapidly growing company.

I loved leaning into my superpowers of *creativity*, *humor*, *humility*, *open-mindedness*, and *playfulness* to find ways for our team to feel connected despite the physical distance separating us. Celebrating holidays and playing games virtually helped us continue to learn more about each other and bond as a team, through fun and laughter. I am grateful for the tools we had available to support us and for my team's dedication to staying connected. These experiences not only strengthened our team bond but also highlighted the importance of connection in our new remote reality, reminding us that teamwork can thrive even in the most challenging circumstances.

GAMBOL SUPERPOWERS

Superpower	Activation
Courage	I lean into my ***courage*** superpower by envisioning the best possible outcome and taking action despite fear. I like to embrace vulnerability as a strength, being open about fears and insecurities while fostering authenticity in myself and others.
Creativity	I embrace my ***creativity*** superpower by cultivating a playful environment through team-building activities and lighthearted interactions. My goal is to foster a dynamic and enjoyable team atmosphere that promotes collaboration and imagination.
Humor	I use light-hearted jokes and a friendly demeanor to lean into my ***humor*** superpower. I like to encourage a relaxed atmosphere where humor is welcomed and appreciated, ensuring everyone feels comfortable sharing funny stories and enjoying lighthearted moments.

Superpower	Activation
Humility	I embrace my ***humility*** superpower by acknowledging my limitations and mistakes, openly admitting when I don't have all the answers or when I've made an error. I am not afraid to look silly or laugh at myself, understanding that infusing interactions with humor and humility fosters a culture of trust, respect, and enjoyment.
Open-mindedness	I lean into my ***open-mindedness*** superpower by actively listening to others' perspectives and respecting their viewpoints, even when they differ from my own. I seek out new experiences and knowledge, remaining curious and open to learning from diverse sources, and embrace change as an opportunity for growth and innovation.
Playfulness	By maintaining a curious and open mindset, approaching challenges with a sense of adventure, and finding joy in the process of learning and discovery, I embrace my ***playfulness*** superpower. I relish in promoting a positive and lighthearted atmosphere where humor and spontaneity thrive.

GAMBOL WRAP-UP

Maya Angelou, American memoirist, poet, and civil rights activist, expertly captured the essence of this chapter with her quote, "Laugh as much as possible, always laugh. It's the sweetest thing one can do for oneself and one's fellow human beings." By embracing your superpowers of ***courage***, ***creativity***, ***humor***, ***humility***, ***open-mindedness***, and ***playfulness*** to have fun with your team, you will create an environment where everyone feels engaged.

GAMBOL REFLECTION

1. Which superpowers really stood out to you in this chapter?
2. Which of these superpowers are most natural for you?
3. Which of these superpowers are most challenging for you?
4. Which story or stories in this chapter did you most relate to?
5. Which story or stories did you least relate to?
6. What fun outings have you experienced with your team?
7. Do you lean into being silly and laughing at yourself? If not, what would happen if you did?
8. What are some ways you can Gambol: Have Fun with Your Team?

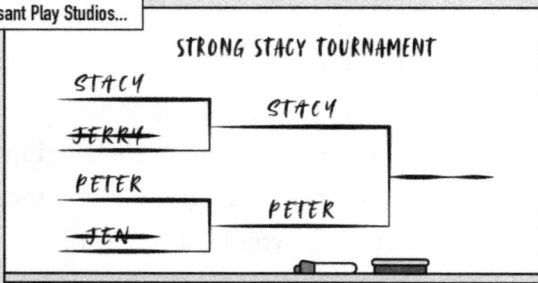

Invincible

Aftershock

"What would you like me to do about my airline ticket?" I asked Ironmind, realizing I would need to let Jessica and two of my other coauthors know I wouldn't be connecting with them during my work trip after all. "Cancel your flight, and if you made hotel reservations already, cancel those too. You will receive a credit for the airline ticket, which you can keep." He said this as if he had just given me a generous gift, for which I should be incredibly grateful.

In the days following my layoff, I was in a state of shock. I shared posts on LinkedIn and Instagram about my layoff and sudden availability, receiving an outpouring of support. I actively searched for my next role, but as I complete this book, I have yet to find it. Over time, rather than becoming more desperate, I have become more selective, applying only to roles that genuinely interest me at companies that appear to have a positive work culture. I then rely on my finely tuned radar during the interview process to spot any signs of the opposite.

We did still qualify for the short-term loan we planned to use until we could sell our house, and we bought our condo later that month. Having no job gave me time to focus on getting our home of over twenty-two years ready for sale. Before putting it on the market I met with our realtor, who was also one of my anthology book ambassadors, and she provided expert advice on what we could do to make it sell quickly. Ticking through her list of improvements took time, but it was well worth it when we received an offer over the asking price two weeks after we listed it. Decluttering was also a lot of work, with too many trips to count to local second-hand stores with hopes that others could benefit from things we no longer needed. We have settled into our condo, with new floors, faucets, and appliances to make it ours, and it feels amazing knowing we have only what we need and we know exactly where to find it.

Looking around our empty house the night we moved out was more emotional than I had expected. I reflected on wonderful memories of moving in, raising our sweet, strong Emma, crazy birthday parties, and huge family gatherings. I suddenly didn't want to leave. The next morning, a quick coffee run after our closing led me by the house, and I caught a glimpse of the new owners taking a photo out front. The dad was running from the camera he had set up on the sidewalk to pose with his family on the front steps. Witnessing their excitement made me smile and took away some of the feelings of melancholy I had experienced the night before.

It was time for another family to turn the page and start their chapter there.

Sharing My Truth

I sat at the small table for two, sipping my iced latte, anxiously waiting for her to arrive. Each time the bell dinged as someone opened the door, I looked up from reviewing the notes I had captured in my phone's Notes app, expecting to see her tiny frame standing in the doorway. Finally, she appeared. I smiled and waved, and she did the same, stopping over to say hi before proceeding to the counter to order her drink.

A few months after our layoff, I reached out to the HR representative who had joined Ironmind that dreadful Monday afternoon to deliver the news to my team members and me. In my message to her, I shared that I had been reflecting on my layoff experience as well as my overall experience at the company, and I asked if she would be open to meeting with me to hear my feedback. Almost two weeks later, I had convinced myself I would never receive a response from her when she surprised me with one. In her reply, she wrote that she had missed seeing my message initially, but was interested in meeting with me.

After ordering her drink, she returned to the table, sat down, and thanked me for reaching out. Then she asked me what I wanted to share. I went through my notes, discussing much of what I have shared throughout this book, first about my layoff experience, then about my working experience with Ironmind and Shadowwit.

I relayed how Ironmind had blurted out the news of our impending layoff to me that Thursday morning, then asked me to keep it to myself until the following Monday. I described the coldness radiating from Ironmind, as well as herself during the meeting, and in every interaction afterward. I conveyed my disappointment in the minimal support my team members and I received, including how I had to ask Ironmind if he had looked into other roles within the company for my team members and if he would be a reference for us. I expressed my confusion about why we were selected while others remained safe. Finally, I shared how hurt we were that there was no mention of us during the all-company meeting where the decision to stop work on the new product was announced. I explained that all of this made it seem like we had been fired, not laid off, and it had rendered us invisible.

Then I moved on to my feedback about working with Ironmind and Shadowwit. I spoke about Ironmind's criticism of me, my team members, and others, and his favoritism towards Shadowwit. I described Shadowwit's fits of rage and how he had shared with me too many times to count that he didn't want to manage people. I expressed my concern about him now managing my two remaining team members. I explained how I felt I had nowhere to turn with my concerns, reminding her of my one and only attempt to seek help when I reached out to her about my unacknowledged quarterly self-assessments. Finally, I divulged how I had typed so many messages to her about Ironmind's C-suite announcement, then erased them, feeling too unsafe to send them.

She listened carefully as I went through my list, asking questions and encouraging me to continue. When I finished, she thanked me for sharing. We chatted for a bit longer, our conversation turning more personal in nature. Then I told her I was writing a book, and much of the feedback I had just shared with her would likely make an appearance. I was expecting her to discourage me, but she didn't.

As we got up to leave the coffee shop, she told me she wasn't sure what would happen with my feedback, but she committed to relaying it to her manager. I thanked her for meeting with me and listening to my feedback, grateful to have reestablished a connection with the warm, caring person I had known prior to my layoff.

"With great power comes great responsibility" is one of the most famous quotes from Spider-Man. As I walked back to my car, I felt lighter and more agile than when I had arrived, like maybe I could swing from a web. I had finally felt safe enough to embrace a great responsibility: sharing my truth. I finally felt seen.

Grand Hike

"Book the flight." I took a photo of the inside wrapper of my Dove Promises Dark Chocolate Almond candy as I savored the rich chocolate square melting in my mouth revealing the small almond pieces hidden inside. I texted the photo to my two nieces JoAnn and Stephanie. JoAnn replied with a heart; Stephanie replied with, "See, Grand Canyon, here we come!" I didn't book the flight that day, but a few months later, after my layoff, I used the credit from my canceled work trip to book it. Then I started training, venturing out onto the hilly gravel roads surrounding our lake home and the river path near our condo, doing my best with the terrain I had to prepare for the intense hike.

The night before our hike, I couldn't sleep. I had finally dozed off after JoAnn and I arrived and reviewed our plan for the next day's hike in detail. I slept long enough to miss Stephanie's late arrival, but there she was, a small outline on the cot at the foot of my bed. In a few hours, we were planning to take a shuttle to the other side of the canyon to hike Rim to Rim, starting on the South Kaibab Trail, down to the canyon bottom to the river, then back up on the Bright Angel Trail, a total hike of 16.5 miles.

I tried unsuccessfully to get back to sleep, replaying the plan in my head and thinking, *What have I gotten myself into? What if I can't do this?* I was relieved when it was finally time to get up and move. I meandered around the room like a zombie, trying to decide what I actually needed to pack for the hike, from the suitcase of things I had brought "just in case." Weighing lack of sleep, limited training, and our later-than-planned start, we debated whether we should stick to our original plan or pivot. I was relieved when we decided on a new plan: hike down and back up the Bright Angel Trail. I didn't want my nieces to be disappointed, but they assured me they were not; they just wanted to spend time together.

As we neared the edge of the canyon and the start of the trail, I felt cold creeping into every part of my body, even though the temperature was nearly perfect for a hike. This was my first view of the canyon, and it was terrifying. We met a group of women planning to do the same hike as us, and they asked us to take their picture. When they were done, we asked them to take ours, and I tried to smile through my terror. "Ready?" my nieces asked. "Yes!" I answered, hoping I sounded more confident than I felt, knowing they could tell I was terrified.

The second I stepped onto the trail, my body froze. The trail seemed so narrow, and I knew the boulders placed along the outer edge would do nothing to prevent me from careening off the side if I stumbled. *I'll just stay over here*, I thought, hugging the canyon wall and trying to make my feet move forward. Each step was a Herculean effort. I knew I needed to move faster, but I couldn't, unable to get over my heights fright. JoAnn and Stephanie were so patient. They didn't push; they encouraged. After several minutes of me making hardly any forward progress, Stephanie asked, "Do you think holding your poles would help you feel more comfortable?" I chuckled and answered, "Well, it certainly couldn't hurt!" Wow! Those poles were a game-changer! Having something to grip with my hands and lean on with each step, instead of tensely clenching my hands at my sides, allowed the rest of my body to relax, and I was able to move forward at almost my normal walking pace. As we continued along the trail, I leaned less and less on my poles, lightly tapping them on the ground as I walked. My focus shifted from how high up I was to how special this time was with my two very strong and brave nieces.

Our plan was to hike down 6 miles to Plateau Point and Trail, checking in at each 1.5-mile resthouse to make sure we all wanted to continue, then hike back up. We reached Mile-and-a-Half Resthouse and Three-Mile Resthouse, and we were all on board with continuing. By the time we reached Havasupai Gardens, the 4.5-mile resthouse, my calves were pretty angry with me about the continuous step-downs, and it was getting hot. I went to use the bathroom and when I met back up with JoAnn, she said, "I am going to head back, but Stephanie is going to continue to Plateau Point and Trail." I was torn, not wanting to disappoint anyone, but after chatting with JoAnn about the climb back up in the heat, I decided to join her. We planned to take our time so Stephanie could catch up and finish with us.

The climb back to the top was hard, 4.5 miles of step-ups, with the first 1.5 miles in almost continuous sun. We took our time, resting in small amounts of shade from trees along the way. We reached Three-Mile Resthouse and I had to sit and rest for a while, then we continued. As we neared Mile-and-a-Half Resthouse, we spotted Stephanie down below and stopped to rest while we waited for her to catch up. JoAnn then decided to go ahead on her own, as she had to deal with a flat tire on our rental car we had discovered right before we left that morning. Stephanie and I finished the rest of the climb together. I loved having time with both of them on our climb down and alone with each of them on our climb up.

On our hike down, we had met people on their hike back up from camping at the canyon bottom and people who were following our original plan. On our hike back up, we took turns passing people as parties rested along the side of the trail. "You waited for me!" I said to a woman we had seen several times as we once again approached her. She smiled an encouraging smile, and it gave me energy. Several minutes later, as we were resting, she caught up to us and asked, "Are you waiting for me?" She looked exhausted. "Of course!" I said with a bright smile, hoping to return some of the energy she had given me earlier, and I watched a huge smile spread across her face. We met up several more times on our long, slow ascent, and each time our interaction recharged me as I hoped it did her. Stephanie and one other brave soul had gone on to Plateau Point and Trail from Three-Mile Resthouse, and I saw recognition and camaraderie in their faces when they saw each other again. Interactions like these, seeing and feeling everyone supporting each other, were the highlights of my day. As I took my final step up, I felt emotional and triumphant, as if I were Batman when he finally made the final leap to escape the deep underground prison known as The Pit in the movie *The Dark Knight Rises*.

That night, I struggled to find a comfortable position in bed as pain surged through my calves, a lingering reminder of the day's grueling hike. As I reflected on my experience, memories of our final stretch washed over me. Each step had felt like a battle, my weary body urging me to stop as vibrant hikers zipped past, full of energy. As I lay in bed, recalling my struggle, a surge of pride swelled within me, masking the pain in my calves temporarily with a renewed sense of strength, as if Ironman's suit had just enveloped my body. Unlike most visitors to the Grand Canyon who only descend a short way before heading back up (likely including some of those vibrant hikers we encountered on our final stretch), we had taken on an intense challenge—one that few dare to attempt. I hadn't just conquered the canyon; I had rediscovered a strength within me that I thought was lost. My layoff had left me feeling deflated and exhausted, but now I felt invigorated and alive again. The hike had served as more than a challenge; it was evidence of my resilience, a reminder that I could overcome any obstacle life threw my way.

The next day, when Stephanie suggested we take on a similar adventure together every year, I didn't hesitate to say "Yes!" despite the intense pain still throbbing in my calves. A few months later, we settled on our next adventure: Every Woman's Marathon, my very first marathon. I felt terrified taking this on but also determined. With proper training, the unwavering support of my strong, brave nieces, and surrounded by many other powerful women, I knew I would push myself to the finish line. And I did!

Tenacious Triad, Reassemble!

I sat holding my phone, trying to decide how much detail to put into my text to Positivity Paladin. I decided to keep it simple and typed, "Hi! How are you? Would you be open to a call sometime this week or weekend? I have an idea I'd like to run by you." He replied almost immediately, telling me he loves his new job, thanking me for being a reference for him, and concluding with, "An idea? That sounds interesting!" I let him know it was about the book I was writing and some potential design work, to which he responded, "Oooooh! Yes! I'm absolutely game."

In a virtual meeting with Jessica the day before, we had discussed the possibility of incorporating a comic strip to support the superhero theme of the book and demonstrate the goal of each chapter. As she and I talked, I immediately thought of Positivity Paladin; he and I had discussed superhero movies and comic books many times while we worked together. I told Jessica I had someone in mind who might be interested and who I knew would do a great job, excited at the possibility of working with him again.

He and I had a phone call that weekend and he was very interested, but I was still in the early stages of writing. I had created an outline and written a couple of chapters, but I still had a lot of details to think through. After a few calls and several emails and texts, he was able to see my vision and came up with the Pleasant Play Studios storyline, which I immediately loved. Then he did some quick character sketches, which I also loved, and when he finally put everything together into the finished comic strip story, he far exceeded my expectations!

During that same virtual meeting, Jessica asked me, "Have you thought about having someone write a foreword for your book?" I shook my head. "No," I said, then asked, "Who typically writes a foreword?" She replied, "Well, often it's someone famous who can endorse the author and their book." I told her I would think about it, and that night I had an idea. The next day I emailed her, "What do you think about me seeing if one of my former team members would want to write a foreword? They could offer their perspective on me as a manager." She liked my idea!

I had plans to meet Stalwart Sage for coffee and Teamwork Titan for lunch the following week. I thought Stalwart Sage, having been one of my book ambassadors for the anthology, might be interested in writing a foreword, so I planned to ask her. But I also wondered if Teamwork Titan might be interested. When Stalwart Sage had to reschedule our coffee, we added her to lunch with Teamwork Titan (a Dynamic Duo reunion), and then we added another former coworker who was planning to move out of the area soon. Over lunch, I shared about my book and Positivity Paladin's commitment to creating a comic strip story for it. I didn't mention the foreword at lunch, but Stalwart Sage and I stayed a bit longer to talk about a potential position they might be adding at her current company, and then we discussed the foreword. We decided to see if Teamwork Titan would want to collaborate on the foreword with Stalwart Sage. After checking with Jessica to make sure a collaborative foreword could work, I reached out to Teamwork Titan to see if she was interested. She was! I was ecstatic! My three original team members, the Tenacious Triad, had just committed to contributing to my book!

The four of us recently got together for lunch as Positivity Paladin passed through Fargo on his way to Minneapolis. On his way back home, we met up again at a theater showing the movie *Inside Out 2*. As I sat in the theater between my former team members, watching Riley's emotions once again work together to help her develop her sense of self, I reflected on how fortunate I am to have worked alongside these three individuals and my other former team members. They gave me grace as a new manager to learn and grow alongside them, and I am incredibly grateful for this experience and for them.

Forging Ahead

In addition to searching for my next role, coordinating our move, training for and completing an intense Grand Canyon hike, writing this book, and training for and completing my first marathon, in my downtime since my layoff I have continued to lean into my Learner strength by pursuing personal development. I signed up for a workshop offered by Nicole Laino on Human Design, a system that reveals your unique gifts and traits based on your birth date, time, and location, learning that I am a 3/6 Emotional Manifesting Generator.

I learned Manifesting Generators are naturally good at lots of things and pick up skills and talents quickly; success comes to Manifesting Generators when they are working with their energy, being playful, and enjoying their lives; and part of their joy is reinventing themselves and moving from project to project. This all makes sense to me, reflecting what I have experienced, but as I learned about the 3/6 Profile, known as the Martyr Role Model, goosebumps started to appear on my arms. As a third line, I am a natural experimenter in life and I learn by doing, often through a process of trial and error. As a sixth line, as I grow older,

I transition into a role model phase where I can offer wisdom I have gained from my experiences to others. I felt as if someone was sending me a message, telling me that I am right on course by writing this book, offering the wisdom I have gained from my years of work experience to others, that this is what I was meant to do.

In this book I have offered my wisdom through The STRONG Framework:

- Study: Get to Know Your Team
- Trust: Let Your Team Know You
- Reinforce: Let Your Team Be Themselves
- Optimize: Let Your Team Shine
- Nurture: Be Your Team's Biggest Fan
- Gambol: Have Fun with Your Team

Sharing real life examples of my experiences as an individual contributor and a team leader, I have demonstrated the use (and at times the absence) of key superpowers related to each of these STRONG goals. If activated consistently, these superpowers will result in creating a work culture where every single employee feels seen, heard, trusted, supported, empowered, valued, and engaged.

In one of my favorite scenes in the movie *Avengers: Endgame*, Spider-Man hands the gauntlet holding the infinity stones to Captain Marvel. "I don't know how you're gonna get it through all of that," he says, looking defeatedly at Thanos's massive army charging toward them. Scarlet Witch lands behind Captain Marvel, followed by Valkyrie and Okoye, one of Black Panther's personal bodyguards. "Don't worry," Scarlet Witch says. "She's got help," Okoye adds. Then Pepper Potts, Wasp, and several other female Avengers land, surrounding Captain Marvel, ready to support her.

Someone once said, "Strength grows in the moments when you think you can't go on but you keep going anyway." I felt invisible after my layoff, but I don't feel invisible anymore. I forged ahead, conquering challenging obstacles while strengthening my mind and my body. I am now embarking on a new writing adventure focused on running and researching a potential new career path: leadership coaching. I now feel strong, and like Captain Marvel, surrounded by people I know are with me and ready to support me, I feel invincible!

Maya Angelou said it best: "People will forget what you said. People will forget what you did. But people will never forget how you made them feel." If you follow The STRONG Framework and lean into the superpowers demonstrated throughout this book, I am confident that you will create a work culture where everyone, including you, feels like a superhero. And maybe, if you're fortunate like me, you will have the opportunity to work with your former team members again, like I have with the Tenacious Triad.

Forge ahead, my superhero friends!

And in the heartfelt words of Tony Stark, aka Ironman, "I love you 3000," because when we lead with love, and lift each other up, we leave a legacy far greater than we realize.

From left to right: Ruth Hetland, Amanda Buth (Stalwart Sage), Alycia Plattner (Teamwork Titan), Nathan Long (Positivity Paladin)

Acknowledgments

This book would not have been possible without the support, guidance, and encouragement of so many incredible people.

First and foremost, I want to thank Jessica Buchanan at Soul Speak Press for believing in this project and guiding it to life with care and expertise. Your insight and dedication were evident at every step, and I am so excited to continue working with you on my next writing project!

To my husband Dale and my daughter Emma, I am sincerely grateful for your love, patience, and encouragement. Your unwavering support has meant everything to me, especially during the late nights and long weekends spent writing and revising. I love and appreciate you both.

To my former managers who bravely demonstrated your superpowers in action, I am truly thankful. You provided me with the tools and inspiration to embrace my own superpowers and build a strong, empowered team. I enjoyed weaving your lessons throughout this book.

To my family and friends, thank you for supporting and encouraging me throughout this project. Your positive energy kept me going when things were overwhelming. To my dear friend who wished to remain anonymous, you have been my sounding board. You listened to my stories and read draft after draft after draft, encouraging me to keep going, even when the path ahead seemed dark, scary, and insurmountable. Your belief in me made all the difference, and I want you to know I couldn't have done this without you. To my nieces JoAnn and Stephanie, thank you for helping me climb into and out of that canyon, rediscovering my strength. I look forward to many more adventures with you!

Finally, thank you to my former team members. I loved working with every one of you, and I hope you saw this reflected throughout these pages. Special thanks to Alycia Plattner (Teamwork Titan), Amanda Buth (Stalwart Sage), and Nathan Long (Positivity Paladin). Alycia and Amanda, my Powerhouse Pair, thank you for the grace you gave me as your team leader, forgiving my mistakes and helping me learn and grow. I am honored that you wrote my foreword, adding depth to the message of this book. Nathan, thank you for enthusiastically creating the comic strip storyline and illustrations, adding such a unique dimension to this work! I loved having this opportunity to work with you again!

This book would not exist without all of you and serves as a testament to how using our superpowers can build a strong team. Thank you for making me feel invincible.

www.ingramcontent.com/pod-product-compliance
Lightning Source LLC
Chambersburg PA
CBHW030516210326
41597CB00013B/934